George Washington

Eminent Lives, brief biographies by distinguished authors on canonical figures, joins a long tradition in this lively form, from Plutarch's *Lives* to Vasari's *Lives of the Painters,* Dr. Johnson's *Lives of the Poets* to Lytton Strachey's *Eminent Victorians.* Pairing great subjects with writers known for their strong sensibilities and sharp, lively points of view, the Eminent Lives are ideal introductions designed to appeal to the general reader, the student, and the scholar. "To preserve a becoming brevity which excludes everything that is redundant and nothing that is significant," wrote Strachey: "That, surely, is the first duty of the biographer."

GENERAL EDITOR: JAMES ATLAS

GEORGE WASHINGTON

The Founding Father

Paul Johnson

EMINENT LIVES

HarperCollins books may be purchased for educational, business, or sales promotional use. For information, please write: Special Markets Department, HarperCollins Publishers, 10 East 53rd Street, New York, NY 10022.

FIRST EDITION

Designed by Elliott Beard

Printed on acid-free paper

Library of Congress Cataloging-in-Publication Data
Johnson, Paul.
    George Washington / Paul Johnson.—1st ed.
      p. cm. — (Eminent lives.)
    Includes bibliographical references.
    ISBN 0-06-075365-X
    Washington, George, 1732–1799. 2. Presidents—United States—Biography. 3. Generals—United States—Biography. 4. United States. Continental Army—Biography. 5. United States—History—Revolution, 1775–1783. 6. United States—Politics and government—1789–1797. I. Title. II. Series.
E312.J67   2005
943.4'1'092—dc22
[B]   2004052907

05 06 07 08 09   ❖/RRD   10 9 8 7 6 5 4 3 2 1

To my American granddaughter

Contents

GEORGE WASHINGTON

Chapter One

A Young Gentleman's Youth in Virginia

As THE CENTRAL ACTOR in the American Revolution, George Washington was one of the most important figures in world history. As America's commander in chief throughout the eight-year struggle against Britain he effectively liberated the thirteen colonies from imperial rule. He then presided over the process whereby the new nation drafted, ratified, and enacted its federal Constitution. Finally, for eight years he directed the administration that put the Constitution to work, with such success that, suitably updated and amended, it has lasted for nearly a quarter of a millennium.

The Revolution he thus led to success was the first of a series that created the modern world in which we live. Its spirit was animated by the same love of representative government and respect for the rule of law that had produced England's unwritten constitution over many centuries. Thanks to Washington's genius, that spirit was successfully transferred to the new American nation. Subsequent revolutions, in France in the 1790s, and in Latin America during the following quarter century, were marred by tragedies of violence and ambition that led to lasting instability, in which the rule of law could not take root. This pattern was repeated, all too often, in the revolutions of the twentieth century, whereby the peoples of Asia and Africa became independent. Throughout this whole period, however, the United States clung to the principles for which Washington fought, and followed during his administrations. They enabled it to survive a near-fatal civil war, to become the world's largest economy, to take in the poor of the planet and turn them into the richest people in history, and finally, at the end of the twentieth century, to emerge as the sole superpower. At the beginning of the twenty-first century, the United States seems set to play the leading part in making the earth secure and democratic. In this immense process, then, Washington played, and still plays, a unique role, both as founding father and exemplar of moderation and wisdom.

What sort of man was Washington, and how did he achieve so much? There ought to be no difficulty in answering this question if documentation alone could supply an answer. For more than a third of his life he worked in the service of his country, and all that he did officially is recorded in the National Archives on a scale no European state could then equal. The American nation-state was born, in public, as it were, and minutely recorded. In addition, from the age of about fourteen, Washington deliberately preserved every scrap of paper belonging to him, including diaries, letters sent and received, accounts, and other day-to-day transactions. As he grew older, he arranged these papers in chronological order, and by name and subject. He seems to have known from an early stage in his career that he would be a figure in history, and he therefore wanted the record to be preserved accurately with the particular object of demonstrating that the offices he held were undertaken from duty, not pride. His overwhelming ambition was to be thought unambitious. His obsession with his papers was thus a strange combination of modesty and self-awareness. He took his archive with him when he went to war, and his personal guard was under strict instructions to protect it with their lives and hustle it to a secret place of safety if the headquarters came under threat. After the war it went to his house, Mount Vernon, and was later hugely augmented by his papers as a president, preserved and sorted by a private secretary and archivist. When Washington died, his assistant Jared Sparks took the entire archive to Boston whence, in 1832, it was delivered to the Library of Congress, which had bought it from the heirs. Mounted, one document per page, hinged at left, and bound in leather, the papers occupy 163 linear feet of shelving, and are sold on 124 reels of microfilm, now on disc. Taken together, they constitute the most complete record of a life in the entire eighteenth century, exceeding by far the vast quantities of memorabilia left behind by James Boswell, for instance, or Horace Walpole.

Despite this, and despite the innumerable accounts of him by contemporaries, and the mountainous literature compiled by historians, so vast that probably no one person can read and digest it,

Washington remains a remote and mysterious figure. He puzzled those who knew and worked with him, and who often disagreed violently about his merits and abilities. He puzzles us. No man's mind is so hard to enter and dwell within. Everyone agreed, and agrees, he was a paragon. But a rich or an empty one? A titan of flesh and blood or a clockwork figure programmed to do wisely? Let us inquire.

The first important fact is that Washington was of impeccable English ancestry and came from the class he admired the most: the independent gentry who owned land. All his life he aspired to behave like a gentleman and to own as much land as he could farm. These gentlemen farmers came from Northampton in the heart of England and were hugely loyal to the monarchy, though Northampton the city, a haunt of shoemakers, is also notorious for producing rebels. In 1657 John Washington, second officer on the ketch *Sea Horse*, of London, sailing to Virginia to pick up a cargo of tobacco, was wrecked on a Potomac shoal, near where Washington the city stands. He decided to settle in Westmoreland County, married Anne Pope, daughter of a substantial man serving in the Virginia House of Burgesses, and so acquired seven hundred acres at Bridges Creek, plus the capital to begin farming. He became vestryman, burgess, magistrate, and militia colonel, helped to suppress Bacon's Rebellion in 1676, and died owning more than eight thousand acres, including an estate at Hunting Creek, higher up the Potomac, said to be twenty-five hundred acres. This became Washington's Mount Vernon, the fixed center of his life, which he personally and meticulously surveyed and found to encompass 2,126 acres.

By the time Washington was born, February 22, 1732, his family had been established for more than three generations and nearly a century, as members of the Virginia elite, self-governing and practicing representative (though not democratic) rule in the English parliamentary tradition. It is important to grasp that Washington saw himself, from boyhood, as part of a ruling class that had run its own affairs as long as anyone could remember, or as the English had always put it, "from time immemorial." Any change, therefore, from without, was usurpation, and to resist it was a moral duty, as well as obvious self-interest.

Washington's father, Augustus or Gus Washington, had ten children by two wives, not unusual in eighteenth-century Virginia, an enthusiastic philoprogenitive colony, whose population increased from 125,000 in 1732, the year Washington was born, to nearly 500,00 in 1775, the year he became commander in chief. Gus, who died when Washington was eleven, was only moderately well off, though he owned ten thousand acres and forty-nine slaves, and operated six iron forges. His household possessions were modest: his silver was worth £125.10 (colonial money was based on the pound sterling till the end of the 1770s) and consisted of eighteen "small" spoons, seven teaspoons, a soup spoon, a watch, and a silver-hilted sword. He had two china tea sets, worth £3.6d, a fine hall looking-glass, a desk or "screwtoire," one armchair, and eleven leather-bottomed chairs, three "old chairs," an "old desk and table," thirteen beds scattered about the house, window curtains, six pairs of "good" sheets, ten inferior ones, seventeen pillow cases, thirteen tablecloths, and thirty-one napkins.

Working in and around the house were thirteen slaves, seven of them "able bodied" (adult and fit). Gus was rich enough, however, to send his sons Augustus and Lawrence to his old school in the north of England, Appleby, which, under its famous headmaster Richard Yates, was the best school in the country. Gus also had his clothes made in England, a practice followed by Washington himself up to the Revolution. Life among the Virginian gentry at that time was simple. Washington's wife, Martha, reminiscing in 1798, said only one family had a carriage, ladies traveled on horseback, and a quarter pound of tea was "a very great present." Gus was a blond giant, and Washington inherited his physique. Otherwise he left little ostensible impression on his famous son. The story of the hatchet and the cherry tree is an invention (1800) by Washington's first hagiographer, "Parson" Weems, a Bible salesman. In the thousands of pages of Washington's personal correspondence, he mentions his father only twice. By contrast, his mother, Mary Ball, Gus's second wife and a wealthy woman in her own right, was a formidable creature whom Washington treated with the greatest possible respect—and reserve. He referred to her publicly as "my revered Mother, by whose Maternal hand (early deprived of a Father) I was led from childhood." A cousin and schoolfellow of Washington's wrote: "Of the Mother I was ten times more afraid than I ever was of my own parents . . . I have often been present with her sons, proper tall fellows too, and we were all as mute as mice." She was "commanding," used to being obeyed.

She was long-lived, being forty-six years a widow, hardy, adventurous, and indefatigable in good family works. Washington inherited from her sound health and the ability to endure great hardships. From his father he inherited his physical appearance. From the measurements sent to his tailor in London and taken after death for his coffin, we learn he was six feet three inches tall. This was, by eighteenth-century averages, enormous. There was nothing gross about him: he was slender, with straight shoulders and wide hips, weighed about 220 pounds, and learned to be a graceful dancer, as well as an enthusiastic one. But his stature was, in a way, the key to his success in commanding men. He never had to shout to be obeyed—except in the noise and heat of battle, when eyewitnesses show him not only shouting but flaying the backs of cowardly officers who were running to safety, using his cane or even a horsewhip (Oliver Cromwell did the same). But, as a rule, his calm, slow, measured—sometimes soft—voice was enough. Benjamin Latrobe, a former aide and highly observant painter, noted: "Washington had something uncommonly majestic and commanding in his walk, his address, his figure and his countenance." Washington's French friend, the Marquis de la Fayette, wrote: "He had the largest pair of hands I ever saw" and could "hurl a stone a prodigious distance." He loved to play baseball, a passion he shared, oddly enough, with his enemy George III (who called the game, English fashion, "rounders"). His stepson Jacky Curtis described his complexion as "fair but considerably florid." His hair, until it lost its color, was red or reddish.

We do not know exactly where he was born. For the bicentenary celebration of 1932 the U.S. Government claimed to have identified his birthplace and the houses he lived in before his settlement at his lifelong residence, Mount Vernon. But such claims are unproven and may be wrong. However, he was certainly born near Pope's Creek, Washington Parish, Westmoreland County. He was called George either after his mother's guardian or (more likely in my view) after George II. Of the years up to eleven, when his father died, we know virtually nothing. His father chose not to send him to his old school in England—probably could not afford it—and Washington, as it turned out, only once left his native America. This was a matter of huge regret to him. He wrote later of "the longing desire, which for many years I have had, of visiting the Great Metropolis of that Kingdom . . . but I am now tied by the leg and must set that inclination aside." In this respect—travel—his horizon was narrow; but less so than that of his antagonist, George III, who never left England, not even to go to Hanover, of which he was king, and who did not even see the sea until he was middle aged.

Instead, Washington was educated within the family or on the estate by one Henry Williams. His notebooks and the evidence of schoolmasters show that in addition to English grammar, he did arithmetic, bookkeeping, geography, geometry, trigonometry, and surveying. His handwriting became, and remained, copybook clear and readable—the neatest of that of any of the Founding Fathers. Thomas Jefferson and John Adams dismissed him as largely uneducated. By his death he had accumulated a library of 734 books, all of which he had bought himself, read, consulted, or dipped into. His formal education was severely practical but well assimilated. Like his younger contemporary Napoleon Bonaparte, Washington was an excellent mathematician with a positive gift for logistics. His accounts were always reliable (unlike Jefferson's which, though copious, often do not add up or make any sense). When John Adams sneered: "That Washington was not a scholar was certain—that he was too illiterate, unread, unlearned for his station is equally past dispute," he misled everyone. Washington's education was in fact well suited, as it turned out, for both civilian and military life. Learning surveying and geography meant that, like Bonaparte, he became an expert map reader, an accomplishment few senior officers in any country possessed; and his logistical skills, acquired in youth, meant he ran his far-flung estates—when he was there—as well as his ragtag army, with growing success, defeating a world power in the field and ending up one of the dozen richest landowners in the country.

It says a lot for Washington's high seriousness when young, and his determination to get on, that after the death of his father, his natural mentor in gentlemen's manners, he acquired and copied out a handbook containing 110 maxims of conduct, originally compiled by the Jesuits, those superb educators of youth, but anglicized and then Americanized in different translations. They included: "Sing not to yourself with a humming noise nor drum with your fingers and feet." "Kill no vermin, as fleas, lice, ticks etc. in the sight of others." "When accompanying a man of great quality, walk not with him cheek by jowl but somewhat behind him, but yet in such a manner he may easily speak to you." This habit of trying to reduce gentility to a set of rules was of the essence of the eighteenth century, as writers such as Tobias Smollett, Benjamin Franklin, and Denis Diderot attest. Indeed, the central fact about Washington's character was that he was Eighteenth-Century Man writ large. He was born in the same year as those two superb exponents of eighteenth-century culture, Fragonard and Haydn. He was a man for all seasons, and ages, but he in no way anticipated the romanticism of the nineteenth century. He did not read Rousseau or any literature after Pope and Addison, whose *Cato* was his favorite work.

But neither did Washington look back to the seventeenth century and its religious zeal. As an adult he became a vestryman as befitted his landed status, but for social reasons. His record of church attendance, about 50 percent or less, suggests decorum rather than enthusiasm. On one occasion he wrote jokingly to his friend Burwell Bassett: "Could you but behold with what religious zeal I hye me to Church on every Lord's Day it would do your heart good." But he was impatient with long sermons and never read religious works. In his twenty volumes of correspondence there is not a single mention of Christ. In no surviving letter of his youth does the name Jesus appear, and only twice thereafter. "Providence" occurs more frequently than God. He was never indifferent to Christianity—quite the contrary: he saw it as an essential element of social control and good government—but his intellect and emotions inclined him more to that substitute for formal dogma, freemasonry, whose spread among males of the Anglo-Saxon world was such a feature of the eighteenth century. It was introduced into the colonies only three years before his birth. The first true Masonic Lodge in America was founded in 1734 in Philadelphia, and Franklin, characteristically, became its Master. Washington became familiar with the externals of Masonry as a boy, and in 1752, when he reached the age of twenty, he was inducted as an Entered Apprentice Mason in the Fredericksburg Lodge. Thereafter, Masonry plays an important, if discreet, part in his life, as it did among many of the Founding Fathers. Indeed, it is true to say that Masonry was one of the intellectual building blocks of the Revolution. Washington allowed lodges to flourish in several of his war camps. It was a link with advanced thinking in France: when Lafayette visited him in 1784, he gave him a Masonic apron of white satin, which the marquise had embroidered. Washington swore the oath of office as president on the Masonic Bible and when he laid the cornerstone of the capitol in 1793 he invoked the lodges of Maryland and Virginia. Indeed at his funeral all six pallbearers were Masons and the service followed the Masonic rite.

There were two other respects in which Washington reflected the deepest instincts of his century: his conviction of the paramountcy of land, and his notion of "interest." He was a soldier and statesman but, above all, he was a landed gentleman. This was what he wished to be; in a sense all he wished to be. There was a saying of his time: "the king may ennoble you but only God (and land) can make you a gentleman." Washington did not like shaking hands, which he regarded as an urban vulgarism, the act of a "citizen," a word just creeping in from Paris. He never thought of himself as a citizen. When greeting you he bowed, and a Washington bow was worth having, a gesture of deliberative elegance. He never wore a wig, which he thought unbecoming and a nuisance, but dressed with great care like a well-to-do English squire, powdered his hair neatly, and tied it with a velvet ribbon called a solitaire. He "looked his land," as they said. He held it to be the central fact of economic life that land was the most valuable of possessions, bringing respect, even power, as well as comfort, and "the commodity most likely to rise in value."

Closely related to actual possessions was "interest." This was another eighteenth-century concept that obsessed him. Interest was a connection, through family ties, friendship, local ties, or clan, which put a man ahead of his immediate competitors in getting something he wanted—a place, a promotion, a contract, a favor. In public service or private enterprise, in the army or navy, in the law, in mercantile deals, it was the key to "getting on," making money, raising your status and income. An exceptional man, such as Franklin, might rise without interest. But for all except the ablest and most industrious interest was essential; without it, a man was doomed to the treadmill of life. Interest also meant motive. It was a term Washington used repeatedly in his letters and other writings. It reflected the lack of sentimentality and idealism so marked in the eighteenth century. He called it "the only bonding cement." He wrote: "Men may talk of patriotism . . . but whoever builds upon it as a sufficient basis, for conducting a long and bloody war will find themselves deceived in the end . . . For a time it may of itself push men to action, to bear much, to encounter difficulties, but it will not endure unassisted by interest." Revolutionary soldiers might enlist from love of their country but they went on fighting only from love of pay and promotion. It was the same with nations. Two nations might act in concert because of a shared ideology but unless they had a common interest they parted company the moment their interests diverged. This was the guiding principle of Washington's geopolitics. It is vital to see that he saw both the Revolution itself and the constitution-making that followed it as exercises driven mainly by self-interest. It was always his dynamic, and he felt no shame in it. Indeed he pursued it relentlessly until his own interest was subsumed in the national interest.

Land and interest: these were the things that mattered. How to acquire them? When his father died in 1743, he left an enormous acreage scattered through four Virginian counties and Maryland. In a complicated will it was divided among his five surviving sons. George Washington, then eleven, received three lots of land in Fredericksburg, two with houses on them, about five thousand acres on Deep Run, shared with his brother Samuel, and his father's own residential farm on the Rappahannock. Washington was never short of acres: the problem was how to exploit them efficiently and make them produce a gentleman's income. His supervision was entrusted to his half-brothers Austin and Lawrence. Both were married with extensive estates, Lawrence inheriting from his father a farm and house on the Potomac that he renamed Mount Vernon, after an admiral under whom he had served in the West Indies.

Lawrence was the most important man in Washington's youth. He had taken advantage of Britain's shortage of officers during the War of the Austrian Succession—following long years of peace under Sir Robert Walpole—to get a regular commission in the army, and though tuberculosis limited his service, he received half-pay until his death. His illness was the occasion of Washington's one trip abroad, accompanying Lawrence to the West Indies in search of sun. During it Washington had a severe bout of smallpox but without any lasting effects, and Lawrence was so grateful for his support that he made his half-brother his residual heir. He also gave the youth his first whiff of heady "interest." This arose from Lawrence's marriage, in 1743, to Anne Fairfax, daughter of William Fairfax, who owned Belvoir, the next estate down the Potomac River. More important, Fairfax was the American agent of the sixth Lord Fairfax, claimant to a vast dominion in the Middle Colonies originally awarded by Charles II. By a decision of the Privy Council in 1745, Lord Fairfax became the owner of 8,100 square miles of Virginia, an area larger than Belgium, extending from near where Washington was born to the sources of the Potomac and Rappahannock Rivers in the Allegheny Mountains.

This legal decision had a fundamental effect on Washington's life. Lawrence's father-in-law, William Fairfax, as agent of these vast Fairfax lands, was clearly a man with interest. For one thing, he had to appoint surveyors, to get the lands mapped, registered in detail, and parceled out. Washington, with his mathematical skills, was already pointing in this direction. Other possible careers had been considered. Joining the Royal Navy as a midshipman was one. A berth was apparently secured for him on a man of war, thanks to the Fairfaxes. Oddly enough, Washington's younger contemporary Napoleon

Bonaparte also considered, as a boy in Corsica, joining the British navy. The reason for rejecting the plan was the same in both cases: lack of interest. It was one thing to enlist as a midshipman; quite another to be "made lieutenant," the first upward step in a naval career. A man might serve as midshipman for twenty years or more if he had no pull with the admiralty. An alternative was to join the merchant marine, and this, too, was considered. But Mary Ball Washington, who disliked the idea of her son going to sea, wrote for advice to her half-brother Joseph Ball, then in England, and his reply (May 19, 1746) was decisive. He wrote that, in the merchant marine, Washington could be in constant danger of impressment, the legal device whereby the Royal Navy manned its ships. The navy would "cut him and staple him and use him like a Negro, or rather like a dog. And as for any considerable preferment in the Navy, there are always too many grasping for it here, who have interest and he has none."

Hence it was decided Washington would begin surveying in earnest. From August 1745 to March 1746, he took a course in the art, and the results survive, both in rough drafts and in fair copies, beautiful and accurate sketch maps of properties that testify to the teenager's industry and enthusiasm. Washington evidently had a natural gift for observing country and getting it down in two dimensions. In 1747, Lord Fairfax himself arrived and the business of examining his vast property, and then his valley beyond it, began in earnest. James Genn, Fairfax's chief surveyor, passed Washington as proficient and he completed his training by an unpaid field internship, under Genn and Lawrence's brother-in-law George Fairfax.

It is at this point, with Washington's first trip from home, to and beyond the mountains, that the teenager—just sixteen when he set out—becomes a real person to us. He began to keep a diary on March 11, 1748, a lifetime habit (with intervals) that survived. It is indicative rather than revealing, showing Washington keen on creature comforts, who took a surprising amount of clothes with him on a trip to the wilderness. (Indeed, there survives from this period, c. 1749, a "memorandum" in his handwriting, giving exact and luxurious instructions on how he wanted a dress coat made.) He notes:

> We got our Suppers & was lighted into a Room & I not being so good a Woodsman as the rest of my Company stripped myself very orderly & went into the Bed as they called it when to my Surprise I found it to be nothing but a Little Straw Matted together without Sheets or any thing else, but only one threaded Bear-blanket with double its Weight of Vermin such as Lice Fleas etc. . . . I made a Promise not to Sleep so from that time forward chusing rather to sleep in the open Air before a fire. . . .

The trip brought Washington into close contact, for the first time, with the Indians—"we were agreeably surprised at the sight of thirty-odd Indians coming from War with only one scalp. The team gave them liquor and it elevating their Spirits put them in the Humour of Dauncing of whom we had a War Dance." He described the motions and the musical instruments in detail, but without comment. It is a significant fact that Washington, then as always in the future, treated Indians as a fact of American life—of which scalping their enemies was merely one feature—rather than an occasion for passing moral judgments, for or against.

There was, however, one central axiom of Washington's view of the world which was already beginning to emerge: the Indians should not be allowed to impede the westward march of American settlement. He never objected to Indians cooperating and sharing in the settlers' superior technology and standard of living. But the idea that the tribes had natural rights in the face of white penetration of their hunting grounds did not occur to him. It was, rather, the white progress into the interior to possess and exploit it using all the resources of their modern agriculture that seemed to him "natural," right, and inevitable.

Indeed, this first venture into the interior made Washington a confirmed westerner. From the very beginning of the European settlement of the American hemisphere, by the Spanish in 1492, two attitudes had emerged among the colonists. One, the majority, was content to take the easy and safer way out, to cling to the coastal strip, exploiting it by planting, exporting the results, and importing all other products, including manufactured goods, from Europe, and by maintaining the closest possible maritime links with the mother country. The other was to move inland, take possession of the entire country, loosen, ignore or, if necessary, renounce the links with Europe, and create an entirely new society, self-reliant, independent, and sui generis. The Latin colonies of South and Central America tended to follow the first course, guided partly by the nature of the terrain, the interiors being mostly inhospitable, and partly by the policies of the home governments, which tried to keep the closest possible control over what the colonists did and where they settled. Hence such cities as were created had their principal, often their sole, links with Europe, rather than with each other. The interior remained to a great extent unsettled. Latin America was thus a littoral or coastal civilization. This character survived the destruction of the Spanish and Portuguese empires, and even the coming of industrialization, and it was reemphasized by the development of a world trading system. Even today many Latin American countries have stronger links economically and in other ways with North America, Europe, and Asia, than with their immediate neighbors. This pattern, this early and sustained preference for the easy way out, explains the comparatively slow and modest development of Latin America. The same pattern was developing in Canada, as a French colony, along the banks of the St. Lawrence, and although French explorers penetrated the Mississippi valley, they did so essentially as emissaries of the French state rather than as individual entrepreneurs determined to settle and build up a new country.

By contrast the English, later British, settlers in New England, Virginia, the Middle Colonies, and the Carolinas, went out under their own aegis rather than under the protection of government. They set up their own representative institutions on English lines and began to run their own affairs from the start. No assistance came from the home government but equally, especially during the first half century, there was no attempt by government to impose detailed control. Governors of the various colonies, though appointed by London, ruled with the consent of the local inhabitants. Moreover, the number of colonists coming out was large, settled permanently, and farmed intensely. In New England, in particular, entire territories were settled, the Indians becoming integrated or moving west.

In Virginia and the Middle Colonies, and farther south, there was a tendency to take the easy way out and settle for a tidewater existence. A planter could raise his crop of tobacco, and load it from his own wharf, by his mansion or farmhouse, directly onto a ship that took it to England. The same ship would bring out goods, both luxury products and basic manufactures. A planter was provided with a catalog and made his order, which was delivered the next voyage out, the ship taking his bale of tobacco in return. This was a primitive but highly convenient system, akin to barter, with everything done on credit. It eliminated the need for large market towns and thus impeded urban development. For the planter it was, again, the easy or lazy way out. But of course it operated very much to the advantage of the capitalist merchant in London, to whom the planter quickly got into debt and remained thus all his life. His heir inherited the plantation, the system, and the debts.

In his letter to his half-sister, Washington's mother, Joseph Ball gave some sound advice about the system. Rejecting the sea, he told her that a planter, if industrious, could live much better than the master of a ship. But she, and her son George, if he became a planter-farmer, must beware. "Neither must he send his Tobacco to

England to be sold [there] and goods sent him; if he does, he will soon get in the merchant's debt, and never get out again." He advised using the market, and being patient: he must "not aim" at "being a fine gentleman before his time." There is evidence that Washington did not exactly follow this advice to the letter. But it made him think; and he was beginning to acquire the practical habit of thinking in the long term, which was the secret of his success in life. The trip to the interior was a stimulant to thought, too. Just as trading exclusively with an English merchant was the easy, and ultimately foolish, way of living, so was clinging to the tidewater lands, and not penetrating even to the piedmont, let alone beyond the mountains, into the vast plains of the interior. As a sixteen-year-old, Washington learned not just the extent of the American interior, but how to judge the quality and exploitability of the land therein. It was already clear that intensive cultivation of tobacco in the tidewater land soon exhausted the soil. Farming had to be improved scientifically or more land— farther west—had to be obtained, preferably both. Washington saw with his own eyes that land, provided one ignored any notional rights of the Indians, was to be had in abundance. But this abundance depended on two things: first, defeating any external threat to possession by foreign governments and their national settlement policies, and second, the absence of any attempt by the home government to interfere with the unrestricted freedom of English settlers to take the fullest advantage of the boundless horizons to their west. The northern and southern boundaries to Virginia had already been fixed by Washington's day. But to the west there was no territorial limit—

unless the French or Spanish governments sought to impose one by force, or the English government to lay it down by law. Otherwise, the western frontier of Virginia stretched right across the continent, until it came to its natural limit on the Pacific Ocean. A land-rich Virginia of vast extent, stretching from the Atlantic to the Pacific—that was the prospect opened up by Washington's first journey to the interior. At sixteen, then, he saw a vision. The next phase of his life was to find him working and fighting against the forces which threatened this vision.

Chapter Two

A Gallant Young Colonel
and His Rich Wife

W ASHINGTON'S LIFE encompassed the period during which the final struggle took place to determine whether the North American continent should be dominated by the Spanish, the French, or the English-speaking peoples. Here was a vast area, much of it superb agricultural land, sparsely inhabited by Indian hunters whose numbers were quickly thinned still further by smallpox as soon as the Europeans came. To grasp its infinite prizes, it had to be mapped and surveyed—but the prizes had to be fought for, too. In both fields Washington was the representative man: as surveyor, his first profession; then as soldier, his second.

Virginia, the first permanent English settlement (1607) had antedated by only a year the first French one in Canada. Thereafter hostilities, intermittent but sometimes intense, had been waged between the two nations in North America for 150 years. The Dutch, once a possible major competitor, had been ousted by the British in 1667, when New Amsterdam became New York. By the time of Washington's birth in 1732, the English held the entire North American coastline from Maine to South Carolina. That year it was extended still farther south, when James Oglethorpe founded Georgia, extending it with the help of groups of Highlanders, Moravians, and Salzburg Protestants. After the declaration of war between Britain and Spain in 1739, Oglethorpe sought to plant the flag still farther by invading Florida, then Spanish. But the attempt failed, and subsequently, during the 1740s, Georgia was threatened by Spanish forces. Spain's empire was in long-term irreversible decline, and the threat to the British colonies from the south was not serious in Washington's childhood and youth. Nevertheless, it was a potential theater of war, depending on the vagaries of European alliances and hostilities.

To the west a more serious threat was developing from the French. Over 150 years they had consolidated their grip on Lower Canada, and founded a colony, Louisiana, at the mouth of the great Mississippi River. Its center, New Orleans, was a viable ocean port, as well as a river one. The British and French had fought over Nova Scotia, or Arcadia, as the French called it. In 1745, in perhaps the most enterprising military action ever taken by an English colony, Governor Shirley of Massachusetts had besieged and taken the great French maritime port of Louisville, which dominated Nova Scotia. At the Peace of Aix-la-Chapelle in 1748, the New Englanders were obliged to hand it back. It was a shock to Washington, then just beginning his career as a surveyor, that the interests of the colonies could be thus sacrificed so wantonly by a British government in Europe, in accordance with its worldwide interests. It was one of the events that pushed him toward the belief that nothing short of entire independence from Europe would suit the true interests of Americans.

The French thus remained a threat in the north. But it was their presence in the west that most concerned Virginia, and so Washington himself. The French never rivaled the English in mass colonization and cultivation of the soil: in Washington's lifetime the population of the British colonies outnumbered all French settlements from Canada to the Gulf of Mexico by ten to one, and the difference increased steadily. But English-speaking colonists were overwhelmingly concentrated into a strip bordering the Atlantic, and were only now, at the time of Washington's first surveying trip, settling the interior. The French aim was to make this restriction permanent by linking up their Canadian territories with the Mississippi valley, claiming the whole of its enormous basin as theirs. They were magnificent explorers, over an enormous area, and worked closely with hundreds of Indian tribes and confederations. They believed in evangelizing them and giving them French civilization. They learned their languages, mapped their territories with astonishing accuracy, and learned their customs. One of their governors, Frontenac, used to meet them painted and dressed as an Indian, something the English found abhorrent. The French priests encouraged intermarriage and there were large numbers of halfbreeds in French territories. The only respect in which the English had an advantage over the French in forming alliances with the Indians was in supplying them with masses of cheap manufactured goods. But this was offset by the rate at which the English propagated themselves: they were exterminating the Indians by sheer density of settlement. Between 1720 and 1750, the period of Washington's youth, total population of the English colonies rose from 445,000 to 1,200,000. This was primarily breeding: the increase based on a high birthrate and good food was twenty-four times the home rate in England, and for the first time travelers noted how much taller Americans were—here, again, Washington symbolized the trend.

Washington himself was intimately involved at a number of levels in the conflict between French and English interests. Expanding Virginia to the west, up to and beyond the mountains, which the surveying and allotment of the vast Fairfax properties involved, brought the settlers into precisely the area on which the French empire-builders were concentrating. This was the vast basin of the Ohio River—the area that linked the St. Lawrence, where the French army was well entrenched, through the Great Lakes, to the main Mississippi Basin, into which the Ohio flowed. For a brief period— Washington's youth—the Ohio River was seen as the key to paramountcy in North America. In 1747 Washington's half-brother Lawrence helped to form the Ohio Company, to promote trade and settlement beyond Fairfax's holdings. Washington's first surveying expedition was part of the company's strategy. But Washington was also employed by Fairfax to intensify the settlement of the tidewater and piedmont areas, and in 1749 helped to lay out the new town of

Alexandria north of Mount Vernon. This was followed by his first formal commission, aged seventeen, as Surveyor of Culpeper County. Under him were a marker and two chairmen. His beautifully neat notebooks survive, signed on each project "G. Washington, SCC." Much of his work was on the frontiers of civilization, and fastidious and orderly as he was—though also capable of great endurance—he objected strongly, in letters and journal, to what he had to put up with, living "amongst a parcel of Barbarians and an un- couth set of People . . . I have not slept above three Nights or four in a bed." He slept on straw or "bairskin" with "Man, Wife, children like a Parcel of Dogs or Catts." The only thing that justified such dis- comfort and ignominy in his eyes was the "Reward." His wages were high, a "dubloon or even six pistoles a day"—that was equal to twenty-two Spanish dollars, and land in the Shenandoah Valley could be bought for a dollar an acre or less. Aged eighteen, Wash- ington began to buy good farm land: fifteen hundred acres in 1750–51. In 1750 Lawrence became president of the Ohio Company, which had half a million acres of "good land" to dispose of.

But Lawrence was already stricken with tuberculosis. At his death in 1752, he left Washington the Mount Vernon estate, subject to his daughter's living (she died in 1754) and his wife's life tenancy. Thus George got the property at the age of twenty-two, and outright in 1760. By his mid-twenties, he possessed about ten thousand acres, not all of it farmed, and was seen as a man of substance. And, as land had to be defended as well as worked, he succeeded his brother also as an officer in the local militia. On November 6, 1752, the able and aggressive Robert Dinwiddie, governor of Virginia, "with the advice and consent of his council," appointed him major and adjutant of the Southern District. He was sworn in before his twenty-first birthday. He was young to hold such rank, though his height, grand appearance, and property assured him obedience. He was given a vital task almost immediately. News reached Dinwiddie that the French were not only in the Ohio valley but were building forts. Their great Governor Duquesne reassured the Indians: "The French make forts and let you hunt under the walls, but the English drive all game away, for the forest falls as they advance." The French even adopted the Indian habit of calling territories "hunts," instead of provinces and counties. All the same, French military activity alarmed the Indians, and careful diplomacy on the English side, assisted by lavish gifts, could ensure their support. Dinwiddie, disturbed by the news about the French forts, petitioned George II in London for permission to take action, got it—plus supplies of ordinance—and instructed Major Washington to lead a military, diplomatic, and intelligence party to the area in October 1753.

This expedition was the making of Washington, both in terms of his self-confidence and in the eyes of his contemporaries. It took place during atrocious winter conditions in wild and mostly unexplored country. He went on horse and on foot, by canoe and hastily made rafts, through rain, snow, and icy rivers, in one of which he was nearly drowned and a companion maimed by frostbite. It involved conciliating suspicious Indians (including "a Queen Aliquippa . . . I made her a Present of a Matchcoat and a Bottle of Rum, which latter was thought the better present of the two"), and discussing the intentions of the French with their commanding officer. Washington found he got on perfectly civilly with the French military, but he concluded that they were adamant in claiming the Ohio valley and could only be removed by force. He examined their principal fort and made a neat and useful sketch map of the entire territory. On his return in January 1754, Dinwiddie got him to write a full report, which was presented to the House of Burgesses, printed, and sent to Europe, where it was widely read and made Major Washington's name as an enterprising and resourceful officer.

As a result, Washington was instructed to recruit men for an expedition to expel the French from the Ohio valley, and at twenty-two he became a lieutenant colonel, in command of a force of Virginia volunteers and Indians, with instructions to build a fort at a river junction called the Ohio Forks, near present-day Pittsburg. He found the French had been established at the Forks for some time and had constructed a stronghold they called Fort Duquesne. He built a rival at Great Meadows, which he called Fort Necessity, an ironic reference to his struggles with Governor Dinwiddie over supplies. He then ran headfirst into an armed French camp under Lieutenant de Jumonville, and when the French ran for their piled muskets, Washington, who kept as usual a diary of events, recorded: "I ordered my company to fire." So shots rang out and his Iroquois Indians also attacked with their tomahawks. Washington halted the killing and accepted the surrender of the remaining French. But by then ten, including their commander, were dead. This incident angered the French deeply; they termed it *l'affaire Jumonville* and treated it as assassination. If Washington had fallen into their hands it is likely he would have had to stand trial for murder. As it was, French retaliation was immediate and on a large scale, leading directly to the outbreak of the Seven Years War, 1756-63, which has been termed the first world war, raging in North, Central, and South America, in the Caribbean and the Atlantic, in India and the East, as well as Europe. Washington got his first taste of fame, as the man who started it. Voltaire wrote: "A cannon-shot fired in America gave the signal that set Europe in a blaze." In fact there was no cannon shot. Horace Walpole in his *History of the Reign of George II* put it more precisely: "The volley fired by a young Virginian in the backwoods of America set the world on fire."

Washington described his first taste of action in a letter to his brother Jack. It found its way into the *London Magazine*, where an unscrupulous subeditor decided to liven up the narrative by enlarging on the author's statement that he was not daunted by the battle: "I heard the bullets whistle and, believe me, there is something charming in the sound." The phrase is highly uncharacteristic of Washington, who took fighting seriously, and it is hard to imagine any real soldier writing it. It infuriated George II, who read the article, and who was very proud of his own active service, especially at the bloody battle of Minden. He exclaimed: "By God, he would not think bullets charming if he had been used to hear many."

In fact the young colonel soon had his fill of hard, hand-to-hand fighting, and tasted the bitterness of defeat not once but twice. On

July 3, 1754, outnumbered and surrounded at Fort Necessity, he was obliged to surrender, but succeeded in extricating his men with their arms: "Soundly beaten," as he put it in his diary. On his return he received the thanks of the Virginia House of Burgesses. His second defeat was in the company of the luckless General Braddock, put in charge of a column of British regulars with orders to take Duquesne. Washington wrote Braddock a powerful letter and, on receiving it, the general put the young but experienced Virginian on his staff with the rank of colonel. The expedition, however, was rashly conducted by Braddock, who was defeated and killed at the Forks. Washington was less critical of the general than others. His conduct, he said, was put "in a worse light than it deserves." But he thought some of the British troops "behaved with more cowardice than it is possible to conceive." By comparison the Virginian militiamen were stalwart. He wrote home: "I luckily escaped without a wound, though I had four Bullets through my coat and two Horses shot under me." He referred to "Our shameful defeat, which really was so scandalous that I hate to have it mentioned." He himself behaved not only gallantly but with great energy and resource, took charge of the remnant, and got them home.

His personal reputation was now such that he was made full colonel and made commander in chief of all the Virginian troops, at the age of twenty-three. He learned many valuable lessons from these experiences, particularly to take defeat in his stride, and to be determined and ready to fight another day. It was vital training for his Revolutionary War experiences. To lose a skirmish or even a battle did not mean you lost the war. Indeed, in this case he eventually had the satisfaction of leading one of the three brigades that took Duquesne (renamed Fort Pitt), destroyed the French forces, and drove them off Virginian territory and out of the Ohio valley. This ended the war, so far as Washington and Virginia were concerned, and he was able to retire with honor. If the British military authorities had had any sense, the victorious Virginian colonel would have been given a regular commission in the British army. If offered, it would likely have been accepted with alacrity, and Washington might thereafter have been employed in defending and enlarging the empire instead of breaking it up. But he had no "interest." So, like Napoleon a generation later, who missed joining the Royal Navy as a midshipman for the same reason, Washington failed to enter the British forces because they did not recruit or promote on merit. Instead, he turned to civilian activities, which he took up with renewed energy.

By the time Washington returned from the French wars, he was a notable figure, a man of evident and rare distinction. We possess a detailed description of him at this time:

> Straight as an Indian, measuring six foot two inches in his stockings and weighing 175 pounds . . . His frame is padded with well-developed muscles, indicating great strength. His bones and joints are large, as are his hands and feet. He is wide-shouldered but has not a deep or round chest; is neat-waisted but is broad across the hips and has rather long legs and arms. His head is well-shaped though not large, but is

gracefully poised on a superb neck. A large and straight rather than a prominent nose; blue-grey penetrating eyes which are widely separated and overhung by a heavy brow. His face is long rather than broad, with his round cheek bones, and terminates in a good, firm chin. He has clean though rather colourless pale skin which burns with the sun. A pleasing and benevolent though a commanding countenance, dark brown hair which he wears in a cue. His mouth is large and generally firmly closed, but which from time to time discloses some defective teeth. His features are regular and placid with all the muscles of his face under perfect control, though flexible and expressive of deep feeling when moved by emotions. In conversation he looks you full in the face, is deliberate, deferential, and engaging. His demeanour at all times composed and dignified. His movements and gestures are graceful, his walk majestic and he is a splendid horseman.

The word "majestic" was often used about him; notably by the architect Benjamin Latrobe: "He had something uncommonly majestic and commanding in his walk, his address, his figure and his countenance. He did not speak at any time with remarkable fluency. Perhaps the extreme correctness of his language, which almost seemed studied, prevented that effect."

Washington impressed men and women almost equally. Having defeated the French—the war in Virginia was virtually over by 1758—he was ready to become a farmer in earnest, and take up his duties as a vestryman, justice of the peace, and burgess. All this, and his need for cash and property to develop his inherited estates, pointed to a prudent marriage, and Washington made one. Martha Dandridge was a rich widow. Her husband, Daniel Parke Custis, had died in 1757, leaving her eighteen thousand acres of land, property worth £40,000, and two small children. She was nine months older than Washington, and tiny by comparison (four feet eleven) with dark brown hair, hazel eyes, a large nose, tiny hands and feet, a soft, rounded woman, talkative, generous, kindly, and efficient in all she undertook. From Washington's accounts, it looks as if his courtship was deliberate rather than fortuitous, and that he set out to woo and marry this valuable and desirable woman, whose assets fitted perfectly into his own. The marriage was not without love, however. The colonel treated her, first to last, as a great lady, and deferred to her on many matters close to his heart and strongly held opinions, for instance on slavery, where her views were more conventional than his, and entertaining, where her expansive, indeed lavish, inclinations were probably irksome to begin with, though he got used to them. She devoted herself entirely to his comfort and career and soon learned to call him "my old man."

The marriage must be rated contented, constructive, and edifying, though in no sense romantic. What it did not produce, however, was children. On this point our evidence is virtually nonexistent. Neither, so far as we know, ever complained. She destroyed all but two of his letters to her, and he kept fewer of hers than might have been expected from a man so costive of documents. There is only one possible clue. Among the hundreds of items ordered from London, many of them for her children, and which included "A child's fiddle . . . a coach and six in a box . . . A stable w' 6 horses . . . Six little books . . . Satten ribbon . . . A Salmon-Coloured Tabby . . . Ruffles to be made of Brussels lace . . . Six pounds (?) of perfumed powder"—there was a mysterious order for a consignment of cantharides. This was the pharmacopoeial name of a dried beetle, vulgarly known as Spanish fly, used internally as a diuretic and stimulant of the genito-urinary organs. It was considered to be an aphrodisiac and might be termed the eighteenth-century equivalent of Viagra. Edmund Burke in his *Reflexions on the French Revolution* was to refer to it: "Swallowing down repeated provocations of cantharides to our love of liberty."

Whether or not Washington swallowed down repeated provocations, no child appeared. But there were plenty of children at Mount Vernon, beginning with his stepdaughter Patsy and his stepson Jacky, both of whom Washington became passionately fond. In due course there were five step-grandchildren and five step-great-grandchildren, not to mention twenty-five nephews and nieces. Washington himself came from a large family that included two married brothers and a married sister, and two cousins who were close: one of them, Lund Washington, looked after Mount Vernon in his absence. Martha, in addition, had two sisters and two brothers, plus various nieces and nephews. So Washington, in effect, had a large family, many of whose members constantly stayed at his house and made it ring with noisy games and childish laughter. He loved children, was at his best with them (and with young women) and his life was never lonely: quite the contrary. Before he became the father of his country, he was paterfamilias of an extended family and loved the role, which he filled to perfection. But his relations were not the only people he had to worry about. Washington all his adult life owned slaves, sometimes scores, sometimes hundreds, and their existence raised for him serious problems, both ethical and practical.

Chapter Three

Slaveowner,
Agricultural Pioneer, Builder

E IGHTEENTH-CENTURY Virginia, in which Washington lived and farmed, was a world in which degrees of servitude were habitual and taken for granted. The highest level of servitude was indentured labor. From the very beginnings, Virginia plantations had been worked by "redemptioners" or "free willers," white immigrants who, in return for passage out to America from England, bound themselves for service for a fixed term, usually two to seven years. This group constituted perhaps 75 percent of total immigration until 1775. A stage below were involuntary workers, also mainly white, who were working off debt or were convicts or "transports," sentenced by British courts to terms of transportation—a minimum of seven years, often fourteen or more—and who were hired out to farmers by the State. The third and lowest group were chattel slaves, black or mulatto, mostly sold to Portuguese slave traders by African kings or chiefs. They were introduced to the British colonies by Dutch traders in 1617 and were soon numerous in Virginia, though it was not until South Carolina was colonized from the West Indies that American chattel slavery became an important institution. However, it is important to grasp that not until Eli Whitney invented the cotton gin in 1793, making possible the mass production of cotton, by slaves, for world markets, that the Deep South came into being, and the South as a whole was hopelessly enmeshed by "the Peculiar Institution."

In Washington's day slavery had not gotten a stranglehold on the South. The first census of 1790 revealed there were 700,000 slaves in the thirteen colonies, 20 percent of the total population, and up to 40 percent in the South. But nowhere did slaves outnumber whites and the institution appeared to be on the retreat. It was made unlawful in England by the Mansfield Judgment of 1772 and two years later Rhode Island followed suit, with Vermont (1777) and Pennsylvania (1780) close behind. It was still possible to believe that slavery might be abolished by gradual manumission, and in peace, and Washington certainly thought so.

Washington always disliked chattel slavery. He thought it morally wrong. His disapproval (hatred is perhaps not too strong a word) increased with age and experience. In 1767 he bought a slave called William Lee, made him his manservant, and taught him to ride. In time Lee became as fine a horseman as his master, and the two rode together, in peace and war, hunting and fighting, as brothers—the general always called him "my fellow," a word carefully chosen. When he eventually gave Lee his freedom (he would have done so much earlier, but that meant losing him, as there was no place for freed blacks in Virginia), he called the act "a testimony for his attachment to me and for his faithful service during the revolution war." Thousands of blacks served under Washington in the war, and he was deeply impressed by their dogged courage and loyalty, and by the refusal of the great majority to take advantage of British offers to free them if they deserted. Washington had no illusions about black slaves, whom he thought poor workers except under the closest supervision. But he could not accept that it was right, as he put it, "to own human beings like cattle."

As a young planter, Washington owned a score of slaves. By his marriage he acquired many more. He also bought slaves in his anxiety to make his estates profitable and pay off debt. He probably had as many as three hundred at one time. A score or so lived in and around his house. Therein lay his second reason for detesting slavery. A degree of intimacy was unavoidable, and Washington was painfully aware of its consequences. There was mixed blood in his wife's family, overshadowed by stories of "Black Jack" Custis. Indeed in his own household there was a black girl called Ann Dandridge, who played with his stepchildren Jacky and Patsy. What they did not know was that Ann was also their aunt, Martha Washington's half-sister. Her father had begot her on a woman of mixed black, Indian, and mulatto origins. Martha kept Ann as a household slave (with her husband's reluctant agreement) because, as with Lee, to free her was to lose her and expose her to an impoverished and risky life in the north. There were many such painful cases. Washington discovered in 1760 that one of his household slaves, who waited at dinner parties, was the unlawful offspring of a prominent local family. "I was informed," he wrote, "that [Colonel Catesby Cooke] was disgusted at my House, and left it because he [saw] an old Negroe there resembling his own image." The slave was the colonel's half-brother.

A further problem for Washington was how to treat his own slaves. Runaways, as with all planters, were a recurrent problem. If you made no effort to get them back, your neighbors were angry; so Washington offered rewards for their return, and his advertisements survive in some cases. Much research has been done on slavery in recent years, using "oral tradition" and other dubious methods. It is said, for instance, that his slaves were badly clothed, but this is contradicted by his advertisements, which describe in detail what his runaway slaves were wearing. Attempts to reconstruct their accommodation at Mount Vernon, and show it to be inadequate, are likewise implausible. We know that Washington drew the line at hunting fugitive slaves with dogs and that he refused to punish them by whipping except in extreme cases. He made efforts to have slaves baptized and educated. At the time of his death, of three hundred slaves on his properties, only about a hundred actually worked. In Latin American colonies, as well as in Africa itself, slaves were habitually worked to death. That was unheard of (and unlawful) in the thirteen colonies. This explains why slaves in the British colonies lived 50 percent longer than those in South and Central America, and twice as long as in Africa, where life for all, slaves or free, was "nasty, brutish and short." Washington did his best to get his slaves to do a reasonable day's work—he himself describes how he used a stopwatch to run an early time-and-motion study of carpenters making fence palings, and set them targets—but his view was that decent treatment produced better results than severity. In this, as in many other fields, he had a keen sense of fairness and justice. He sold slaves very occasionally but never in a way to break up families. A particularly unpleasant piece of modern "research" has Washington supplying himself with false teeth by having them extracted from the mouths of slaves and transported to his dentures, by an itinerant French dentist who visited Mount Vernon. In fact his false teeth were chiefly of hippopotamus ivory, occasionally wood.

Washington also disliked slavery because he considered it economically inefficient and the incorrigible enemy of good farming. It tied Virginia planters to their own form of slavery—one-crop tobacco planting. This system was made for lazy, self-indulgent landowners. Tobacco, especially in the tidewater, was labor intensive, involving endless hoeing carried out by slaves. Four times a year or so, a ship from England tied up at the estate jetty (all had them), and the bales of tobacco were taken aboard. The ship also landed English-made goods, luxuries or necessities, ordered by the planter on its last call. The London agent sold the tobacco on the European market (there was none in Virginia) and put the proceeds against the cost of the goods he supplied. The planter really had no control over the process and, with rare exceptions, planters were always in debt to their London agents, sometimes (as in Jefferson's case) disastrously so. This system was one reason for underlying anti-British feeling in Virginia. The system only worked at all because of slavery, and Washington detested it. Indeed it is one of Washington's strengths that he not only denounced the system but did everything in his power to replace it, on his estates, with modern, efficient farming.

Once the French and Indian War died down in Virginia, in 1760, and Washington began to run his estates in earnest, he took scientific farming seriously. He was an active man, who loved being on horseback—and often was, from dawn to dusk—and he had a tidy, methodical mind, enjoyed acquiring knowledge by experience, and delighted in a complex, difficult business that was, by its nature, creative. When he wrote about farming, he became almost eloquent:

> I think that the life of a Husbandman is of all others the most delectable. It is honourable. It is amusing. And with Judicious management it is profitable. To see plants rise from the Earth and flourish by the superior skill and bounty of the labourer fills a contemplative mind with ideas which are more easy to be conceived than expressed. The more I am acquainted with agricultural affairs the better I am pleased with them. I can nowhere find so great satisfaction as in those innocent and useful pursuits.

He concluded that it was "delightful to an undebauched mind [to make] improvements on the earth."

But how exactly, in his case, were these "improvements" (a typical Washington term of approval: he wanted no utopias or violent transformations; merely a change for the better) to be brought about? The first thing was to get away from single-crop planting. He never had any real success with tobacco, either as a bachelor working his inherited land or as a married man running the Custis estates. He recognized that tobacco had, in the seventeenth century, been the making of Virginia, but he disliked smoking and thought raising poor-quality tobacco (the only kind now possible in the exhausted tidelands) a formula for idleness and debt. Indeed tobacco farming had gotten him into debt. He was in debt before his marriage, and in his efforts to reorient his entire estates to mixed farming, he not only got through the cash reserves and audit of the Custis inheritance but contracted further debts, or so he complained in his letters. However, Washington's frequent references to indebtedness in his correspondence at all periods of his life should not be confused with insolvency. The great majority of landowners, on both sides of the Atlantic, but especially in America, with a primitive or nonexistent banking system, and a chronic shortage of notes and coins, were technically in debt. But this is what we would now call a problem in cash flow rather than improvidence. At no time in his life did Washington's liabilities exceed his assets. On the contrary, especially after he married, he was extremely asset rich, and his borrowings to provide working capital were only a tiny proportion of his net worth.

Washington's object in recapitalizing his farming business (to some extent on borrowed money) was to undertake large-scale agriculture on the new English model. Then and always he admired things English (with notable exceptions). England was going through an agricultural revolution, thanks to the work of such innovators as "Turnip" Townsend, Jethro Tull, and Coke of Norfolk: their improvements were to make it possible to feed the offspring of the demographic revolution that was just beginning, and to enable the industrial revolution, the first hints of which were apparent, to take place and transform the world. The population of the American colonies was growing, thanks to spectacularly high birthrates and immigration, even faster than Britain's was. How were these teeming mouths to be fed?

The answer, as Washington saw it, was to expand inland to the rich agricultural land he had examined on the far side of the mountains, and to work it with modern English farming methods. In the 1760s Washington had about twenty thousand acres in hand. Many rich English earls and dukes had no more. Whence the difference in their income and his? It was because the best English farming was a judicious mixture of arable, pasture, and stock raising, all for the market. He noted that, whereas tobacco had to be marketed overseas, with the growth of American cities, especially New York, Philadelphia, and Baltimore, a big and growing market in foodstuffs already existed. So his first move was to shift to wheat production. This meant investment. One reason why Washington was in debt, even more so after his marriage than before, was that he was putting money into land and livestock (including able-bodied male slaves) as he switched from planting to farming. Wheat was less labor intensive than tobacco—a skilled ploughman could do the work of forty slow-hoeing slaves—but it demanded large numbers of draft animals, and they in turn needed large quantities of hay. So he planted corn fodder as well as wheat, he raised root crops and experimented with such forage crops as clover and alfalfa, and he also put out fields for cattle and hogs. They in turn, and his plough horses, produced manure, which he used as fertilizer. He grew peas and potatoes, planted vines, and set up fruit and vegetable gardens not only at Mount Vernon but in all his farms. He detailed seasonal, weekly, and daily work procedures. He became an expert in many tasks: wheat threshing, fruit tree grafting, sheep shearing, fishing for herring, and dragging for sturgeon. "I begin my diurnal course with the Sun," he wrote, to make sure "my hirelings" were at work shortly after. Having ensured that "all Wheels were in motion," he breakfasted at seven o'clock. Thereafter he was "riding round my farms, which employs me until it is time to dress for dinner."

It is clear he enjoyed routine. But there was play, too. Washington hugely enjoyed fox hunting—he was a "thruster," especially after he acquired William Lee to thrust with him: "the two men would rush at full speed through brake or tangled wood in a style at which modern huntsmen would stand aghast." We know the names of some of his favorite hounds: Jupiter, Tartar, Tippler, Trueman. In the season he hunted three times a week, but he also walked "several miles" after dinner, to keep fit. He performed all the social and representational duties appropriate to men of his rank, from vestryman in the church to sitting in the Virginia House of Burgesses, which had been in existence, when he joined it, for nearly 150 years, performed most of the normal functions of government, and seemed as solidly part of the natural order of things as the parliament in Westminster itself. He and Martha also entertained. Between 1768 and 1775, they had to dinner more than two thousand people, most of them (as he put it) "people of rank."

In order to carry out such social duties properly and amply, Mount Vernon had to be transformed from a farmhouse into a Palladian mansion, not as grand indeed as those now appearing all over England, but of a similar general appearance. It is true to say that Mount Vernon, the house and estate, and the family that lived in it, were the most important things in Washington's life by far. First and last, they dominated his thought, gave purpose to his ambitions, and animated his patriotism and public service. Mount Vernon, as a home and farm, went back to the seventeenth century as a Washington possession. They became his in 1754, and his outright property in 1760. But it was from his marriage in 1759 that he began to improve and extend and beautify the house itself. He never had an architect as such, but he had handbooks and craftsmen. He liked to learn about house improvement and do things for himself.

The extension of the farm into a mansion house began in 1759 and continued until Washington's death and beyond. As with Jefferson's Monticello, it was never finished until it began to fall into ruin, many years after the great man was in his grave. Much of the work was carried out during the Revolutionary War and Washington's presidency. There were always craftsmen and builders at work, and Martha had to put up with it. The site of Mount Vernon, on its bluff overlooking the creek, where quite large ships came to anchor and tie up, was and is magnificent, and Washington's aim was to build the mansion so that its owner could look out on and enjoy the prospect. So he extended the original box by adding wings, topping them with another story, and then (when he was already president) pulling it all together by a grand portico or loggia running the entire length of the extended house.

The earliest structure on the site, c.1698, probably had only two rooms. The farmhouse Washington inherited, built by his father in 1735, had four. The mansion, as extended by Washington, eventually had eighteen main rooms, plus fourteen auxiliary buildings, including the kitchen, which was not in the mansion. The new rooms included a large entrance hall, a library with the master bedroom above it (equipped with the exceptionally wide bed, six and a half feet long, on which Washington insisted), and a large banqueting hall with a Palladian window, furnished only after the war. The roof was crowned with an octagonal cupola, and the mansion was surrounded by formal gardens, laid out by Washington, a large walled kitchen garden, a smokehouse and greenhouses and, not least, a bowling green for stately games after dinner.

Washington paid great attention to detail, using handbooks on architecture and decoration. It was his idea to put up the loggia. He also devised an outer cladding for the enlarged house, consisting of yellow pine siding, grooved blocks of granite to resemble "rustication," covered in several coats of white paint mixed with sand to give it the rough texture of stone. So the sides of the house were off white, in contrast to the roof of thick colonial shingles of reddish brown, brown doors, and green shutters. One visitor, Latrobe, described it as "like an English gentleman's house of seven or eight hundred a year."

The internal decorations were also Washington's work. He insisted on the best, particularly in his study, which was linked to his master bedroom above by a private stair, and was next door to the private dining room. The study had a Windsor fan chair, a swivel-seated desk chair, made by Thomas Burling of New York in 1790, and eventually a new secretary-desk made by John Aitken of Philadelphia in 1797. George Washington Parke Custis, who was raised at Mount Vernon, said the study was a place where no one entered "save by direct order"; it was "very handsome" with total privacy, necessary in a house where 'perpetual and elegant hospitality was absolutely required." Washington was still giving orders about the banquetry room from his camp during the war. But he was able to supervise personally the decking out of his private dining room, 1757–60, and 1775, which he chose from Abraham Swan's *British Architect*. He employed two fine craftsmen to follow the schemes described therein, Bernard Sears as the wood-carver, and a French *stuccatoro* (name unknown) for the plasterwork.

Always an admirer of things English, when they were well done, Washington got ideas for the embellishment and running of his house from the Williamsburg mansion of Lord Botetourt, governor of Virginia, where he often dined. He learned from the governor how to treat staff and how to conduct ceremonial interviews. The governor had twenty-five indoor staff under a remarkable English butler, William Marshman, whose pantry was superbly equipped, and is beautifully preserved. So, of course, is Mount Vernon, after many vicissitudes in the nineteenth century. About 70 percent of its original furniture and fittings have been recovered and put in place, plus many other treasures. Martha Washington had a special tea service made and had a charming habit of presenting favored house guests, on their departure, with a cup and saucer from the set. Many of these have been given back by descendants of the guests.

All in all, Mount Vernon as it is today gives visitors an accurate impression of the "little paradise" that Washington and his wife created. With its superb views, dignified exterior, and carefully planned comforts, and its far-flung network of farms and demesnes, it formed one of the most desirable estates in America, and was one of the best run. Had Washington not been twice called to public service, each time for eight years, and been able to devote his life to working up his lands and adding to them, it is likely he would have achieved distinction as one of colonial America's most far-sighted and successful farmers. As it was, despite absences and distractions, his property at his death had become worth over half a million dollars, making him one of the country's richest men. However, much as he loved Mount Vernon, he loved America more, and the time came when he felt obliged to devote himself to its service body and soul.

Chapter Four

Commander in Chief and Victor

A S A LEADING landowner and a Virginia burgess who sat upon the House's key committees, Washington was involved in the dispute with Britain from the start. But he was never a militant or an agitator, let alone an extremist. He saw the issues clearly enough but he was reluctant to draw the logical conclusion, that separation was inevitable. As late as October 1774, when the colonies were already forming governments to assert their rights, Washington wrote (to Captain Robert Mackenzie): "I think I can announce it as a fact, that it is not the wish or interest of that government, or any other upon the continent, separately or collectively, to set up for independency. I am as well satisfied as I can be of my existence that no such thing is desired by any thinking man in all North America."

Nevertheless Washington was always clear in his mind that a high degree of self-government must be exercised by the colonies, as indeed it always had been. He saw the House of Burgesses, functioning for a century and a half with great success, under the loose rein of a royal governor (appointed with its approval) as the proper ruler of Virginia. Like most other Americans, he saw the assertion of power by the British government, after the end of the Seven Years War, as a usurpation, an innovation, and a suppression of rights enjoyed by the colonists from the beginning. This point was brought home to him in striking fashion as early as October 1763 with George III's proclamation reserving all trans-Appalachian territories to the Indians. The king's military advisers had pointed out to him that one of the most important lessons learned in the war was the need to keep the allegiance of the Indian tribes in any future conflict in North America. That meant treating them as British subjects, not exactly on a par with the white colonists but with the same right to look to Britain to protect their fundamental interests, above all the integrity of their hunting lands. Accordingly the king's proclamation read: "We do hereby strictly forbid, on pain of our displeasure, all our loving subjects from making purchases or settlement whatever, by taking possession of any of the lands above reserved, without our special leave or license for that purpose first obtained."

This royal decree struck directly at Washington's personal interests. It contradicted an earlier proclamation of 1762, when the war was still raging, which allocated, free, hundreds of thousands of acres of western lands to veterans of the war. He was not only a beneficiary of this donation but hoped to obtain much more than his nominal share of it. A letter to his brother Charles survives in which he shows his anxiety to acquire allocations to other veterans. It reveals a devious side of Washington, which was not, on the whole, a central part of his character but which tended to creep out when real estate was at issue: "As you are situated in a good place for seeing many of the officers at different times," he wrote, "I should be glad if you would (in a joking way, rather than in earnest at first) see what value they set upon their lands . . . if you should make any purchase, let it be down in your name, for reasons I shall give you when we meet. In the whole of your transactions, either with the Officers or in this other matter, do not let it be known that I have any concern therein . . . show no part of this letter."

There can be no doubt that, but for the Revolutionary War, Washington would have become a major landowner in trans-Appalachia. Few knew more about it or had a stronger belief in its unlimited future. And his interest was not merely personal but national. He was an early believer in what was later defined as Manifest Destiny. Virginia's western frontier must eventually be the Pacific. The relish with which he used the word "continental" meant he saw colonies eventually encompassing all of North America. The king's decree, if enforced, made that impossible. Moreover, it seemed to put Indians and settlers on a legal par. Unlike many colonists, Washington did not hate Indians. He always treated them with respect. But he also regarded the tribalized Indian as a savage, a word he habitually used when referring to them. He did not exactly state that, unless they detribalized themselves and mingled with the settled population (as many did), they had no future in America. But that is what he clearly thought. The expanding colonies could not live side by side with sacrosanct Indian hunting grounds. Hence King George's decree was a denial of America's future.

To Washington, the sealing of the open frontier to the west was the fundamental reason for resisting Britain, but it was also symptomatic of the conflict of rights between colonial assemblies and Westminster. This was brought center stage by George III's Declaratory Act, passed by the Westminster parliament three years later: "The said colonies and plantations in America have been, are, and of right ought to be, subordinate unto, and dependent upon, the imperial crown and parliament of Great Britain."

Washington was always clear that if this act was enforced in full, then America would have no alternative but to resist by force, though as late as 1774 he believed Britain would compromise, retaining theoretical rights but leaving the colonies with the reality of decision making. The issue of taxation was, of course, part of this conflict of rights though not, to Washington, the most important part. The truth is, though he liked the two governors of Virginia he knew, Dinwiddie and Botetourt, Washington had a low opinion of the London government and its ability to take the right decisions affecting America. His compatriots hated any kind of taxation, and it is one of the most important facts in the country's history that America remained a low-tax country until the second half of the twentieth century. Washington did not wholly share this opposition to taxation. As a soldier he knew that armies were necessary for a country's security. They had to be paid, and that meant taxes. As president he was to insist that regular forces were essential and his ruthless suppression of the Whiskey Rebellion showed his insistence that taxes be paid by all. But he thought, in the 1760s, that taxes paid by Americans should be determined by them, in the interests of efficiency as well as equity.

Hence he thought the 1765 Stamp Act, which began the process of separating America from Britain—as he wrote, to his London agents—not only "unconstitutional" and "a direful attack upon [our] liberties," but impracticable: "our Courts of Judicature will be shut up, it being morally impossible under our present Circumstances that the Act of Parliament can be complied with." There was simply not enough cash available for most people to pay the stamps. It would have a disastrous effect on trade with Britain, and British merchants would suffer most. When the act was repealed, Washington thought the 1767 duties imposed by Charles Townsend instead to be even more ill judged. They had the effect, as he pointed out, of raising the prices of imported British goods even higher than they were, and that was too high, because Britain was yet to embrace free trade (which did not happen until the 1780s) and was still an old-fashioned mercantilist country that forbade its colonies to trade freely in international markets. Washington foresaw that the duties would have the effect of turning Americans against trade with Britain, increase smuggling of commodities and, with manufactures, persuade Americans to make their own, thus accelerating a process which was beginning anyway. As he predicted, the response of the colonies to the new taxes was a boycott, in which he conscientiously joined, and a boost for local business, of which he strongly approved. From first to last, Washington wanted America to have an all-purpose, rounded economy, with its own markets and financial system. He never shared the views of some of the Founding Fathers that it should be dominated by Roman-style rural patricians, running their estates in conjunction with running the country.

Washington was baffled and in the end angered and disgusted by the sheer ignorance and incompetence of the home government from 1763 onward. Brought up to admire things British and full of admiration for the small country that had won the first world war in history, he could not understand what was happening in London. The speed with which George III got rid of the men who had won the Seven Years War was extraordinary, exceeded only by the stupidity or improvidence of those he appointed in their place. The Earl of Bute, his first prime minister, was a mere favorite. Charles Townsend, "Champagne Charlie," as he was known, was an epileptic, an eccentric, and a man of rapidly changing impulses. He designed his disastrous duties and imposed them almost without forethought or preparation—he was probably already a dying man. Lord George Germaine, the Secretary for the American Colonies— a true colonial office did not come into existence for another generation: that was part of the trouble—was a disgraced officer, convicted of cowardice at the Battle of Minden (the great Pitt, now in bitter opposition, had directed that the sentence be read out in front of every regiment in the army), and had been pronounced "unfit to serve His Majesty in any capacity." But he was sycophantic and the new young king, who liked subservience, brought him into office where, in contrast to his previous timidity he displayed a bellicosity toward America that was wholly misguided. The Earl of Sandwich, in charge of the navy, insisted on deploying most of it in European waters, believing America of no importance, and in addition starved it of funds—in which he was at one with Lord North, another of George III's boobies, who had a passion for economy and a dislike for reading his papers—he was slowly growing blind.

Washington, like most Americans, believed at this stage that the London ministers were to blame for the mishandling of America and that the king was blameless. He gradually came to realize the truth: George III, his royal arrogance, his ignorance, stupidity, and above all obstinacy, were at the root of the problem. George did not even learn to read until he was eleven, and at twenty his writing was still childish. His inability to understand any viewpoint but his own was incorrigible—he quarreled with all his sons and kept his unfortunate daughters in nunnish isolation from the world. He eventually went incurably insane, and there are hints of unreasonable behavior throughout his life. What Washington could not understand was why none of those who held power on the British side made any attempt to learn about the American people, their history and views. None of them grasped that the colonies had had representative governments since their inception, in some cases going back six generations. Those familiar with both sides of the Atlantic, such as Benjamin Franklin, were quite sure that a compromise was possible if only the two sides met and talked. Washington's practice, as a landlord of scattered territories, was to inspect them personally, and hurry to any trouble spots. He could not understand why no one from London came on a ministerial visit. Of course George III should have come himself. A royal visit might have made a vast difference. But George, unlike his forebears, never went anywhere. He did not once visit even his continental territory, Hanover, of which he was elector. He never left England. He lived almost entirely at Windsor, going to London only for formal engagements. He thought he could do everything by tête-à-têtes with individual ministers, and by writing letters. Oddly enough, if he and Washington had even met, they might have gotten on splendidly, for (in addition to baseball) they had one passion in common: agriculture. The King was not called "Farmer George" for nothing.

As it was, events drew the two men into one of the longest wars in the history of either of their countries. Though Washington had had a brilliant military career as a young man, he had not carried much political weight in Virginia—his first two efforts to enter the House of Burgesses, in 1755 and 1757, were failures. He got in for Frederick Curt in 1758 and from 1765 from his home county, Fairfax. But as the picture darkened in the 1760s, his influence, as a man of action, increased. When Governor Botetourt dissolved the assembly in 1769, for its assertion that Virginia had the right of self-taxation, Washington was among those who took part in an unlawful session of it in a tavern. He was elected to the committee that voted a boycott of British goods—the Nonimportation Association. This had the desired effect. The Townsend duties (except those on tea) were repealed in 1770 and the association dissolved the next year. Washington was able to attend to his own affairs. He took a leading role in securing the Ohio bounty to which his wartime service entitled him, and bought up the rights of other officers, eventually in 1773 securing more than twenty-four thousand acres.

His acreage took him deep into western Virginia (often by canoe), and he devised a plan to improve navigation on the upper Potomac; he was already involved in a plan to drain the Great Dismal Swamp on Virginia's border with North Carolina. He also opened a commercial flour mill at Mount Vernon, and businesses involving weaving and sea fishing. However, in 1774 the closing of Boston Harbor in retaliation for the Boston Tea Party reopened the conflict in a more acute form. The Virginia Assembly was again dissolved, and again re-formed unlawfully; Washington called with others for "a general congress" of the "several colonies of British America" and he presided at a meeting that adopted the "Fairfax Resolves," calling for self-government and an intensified boycott. He was one of seven Virginian delegates to the First Continental Congress, which asserted the right of colonial legislators to an "exclusive power of legislation . . . in all cases of taxation and internal policy."

This entry of Washington into national politics was confirmed in March 1775 when he again represented Virginia at the Second Continental Congress. By now the war had begun in Massachusetts, with fighting between the local militia and British forces at Concord and Lexington on April 19. He had attended the first Congress in Virginia and at the second, in uniform, he was greeted in Philadelphia as commander of five Virginia militia companies. He left Mount

Vernon on May 4, in his blue and buff uniform, and was not to see his home again until a brief visit on his way to Yorktown in 1781.

The circumstances in which, at the second Congress, Washington was chosen commander in chief of the Revolutionary forces, merit a brief analysis. He was a good, even obvious choice. But he was not the only candidate. His appearance in uniform at both Congresses, which he himself felt was a token of the seriousness with which he took events and his belief that a trial by force was now inevitable, could also be seen as a job application, for the towering figure in his regimentals was certainly the most impressive at that gathering, especially now it was turning from verbal protest to action. The choice was unanimous. But then, as always, Washington was an impenetrable mixture of ambition and diffidence, of confidence and self-doubt.

When the invitation was made public on June 16, 1775, he told Congress that he felt "great distress from a consciousness that my abilities and military experience may not be equal to the extensive and important trust." He added: "I beg it may be remember'd by every Gentn. in the room, that I this day declare with the Utmost sincerity that I do not think myself equal to the Command I am honoured with." Two days later, in a fine and touching letter to Martha, telling her that he must proceed immediately to Boston to take over the army, he insisted "so far from seeking this appointment I have used every endeavour in my power to avoid it." But he recognized "a kind of destiny that has thrown me upon this Service"—and he hastened to go on to practical matters, such as his bringing his will up to date, and the dispatch of material to her for a dress, giving the cost, a typical Washingtonian communication.

The general took up his command at Cambridge, Massachusetts, on July 3. The Continental Army, mostly on short-term engagements for militia regiments, numbered fourteen thousand. It dwindled to ten thousand by the end of 1775, as terms expired. From first to last, in an eight-year war, Washington never commanded more than sixty thousand in all (subject to a 20 percent annual desertion rate), and his force in battle was never more than ten thousand, usually much fewer. He was short of everything: virtually no guns, to begin with, little small arms ammunition, few uniforms (it took him three years to create a uniformed force and five to persuade his officers to adopt uniform rank badges). There was a shortage of blankets and tents (it was a year before he acquired one blanket apiece for his men). There was little money, sometimes none. Washington himself served without pay, claiming only his carefully accounted expenses. But the men needed to be paid and often were not. There were various mutinies, all chiefly about arrears of pay. There was virtually no discipline and the officers (mostly elected by the men) were incapable of enforcing it. Washington eventually secured from Congress extraordinary legal powers, under courts martial, and though a genial and kindly man, did not hesitate to try and execute by firing squad the worst offenders.

Equally important, Washington also secured the services of a German veteran, Friedrich Wilhelm von Steuben, who devised uniform drill—essential for keeping formation under fire—trained drill sergeants, and got the routine discipline under control. He also found in Henry Knox, a former Boston bookseller—and a man as tall as himself, though much heavier—an artillery man of genius. During the winter of 1775–76, he formed in Ticonderoga and transported over trails in the Berkshire Mountains and across the Hudson River a number of cannon and, by deploying them atop Dorchester Heights, compelled the British to evacuate Boston in 1776. Knox's cannon were also decisive at Yorktown. Finally, in Alexander Hamilton, a lawyer from the West Indies and a fierce and brilliant field commander, Washington discovered a superb chief of staff from 1777 to 1781 (his nominal position was secretary), who presided over a score of aides-de-camp, half of them Virginians. These young men, each ranked a colonel, he called his military family, the martial equivalent to his personal family at Mount Vernon. He treated them with love and tenderness, and they worshipped him and (with one or two exceptions) served him with fanatical loyalty. Thus Washington, entirely as a result of his personal qualities—not too much to say his charisma—possessed, for the first time in history, a first-class general staff, who understood his mind and methods and could carry out his intentions religiously. This was something none of the British commanders had; indeed, it was denied to the two outstanding generals of the next generation, Napoleon and Wellington. But, in strict military terms, it was all Washington had. In all other respects he was outnumbered, outgunned, and outfinanced. (One of his opposite numbers, Sir Henry Clinton, lived on his expenses, banked all his handsome pay, and returned to England defeated but a rich man.)

Washington will never go down as one of the great field commanders. He was not an accomplished tactician and rarely trusted himself (or rather his men) to maneuver once battle began—though he was always hyperactive himself, riding about and whacking with his sword both enemies and cowards among his own troops. Of the battles he fought, he lost three out of ten. On the other hand, he was a strategist of genius, who understood very well what kind of a war he was fighting and how to win it.

Washington started with a fundamental conviction: that America's cause was not merely just, morally, but legitimate in a legal sense. The colonies—now states—had been self-governing since their inception and delegation of power by their peoples to legislative assemblies. Britain's assertion of power, as in the Declaratory Act, was *ultra vires* and a usurpation, and resistance to it not merely lawful but a moral obligation. He never deviated from this belief, which was the ultimate source of his energy and determination to win, especially when times were bad. It followed from this that Congress was a legitimate government, as entitled to obedience and internal respect as Britain's own, that the army was its duly constituted military arm, and that he, as its commander in chief, was as possessed of all the rights as any field marshal of a great European power. That is why, in correspondence with British commanding generals over treatment of prisoners, he not only insisted on reciprocity—Americans held by the British were never to be treated as rebels but as POWs, just as he respected the martial rights of his prisoners—but also that he was addressed in letters as "General Washington":

otherwise he refused to receive them, and he won his point.

At all costs, Washington was determined to preserve the congressional government and the army as its instrument, and never to lapse into guerrilla status. He was convinced, rightly, that if he kept in being the American government and army long enough, the British, tired of the war, would recognize their existence, this being the prelude to negotiation, which must end in independence. He therefore fought a war of endurance and attrition, avoiding pitched battles except when circumstances were overwhelmingly in his favor, unworried by defeats so long as he kept his army together and the government, in effect, ruling the country.

The British strategy was the logical opposite. Congress had no legitimacy, the army was a band of rebels, and Americans, however organized, could never be more than *subjects*, with no more collective rights than Indians. The king and his government, therefore, always insisted that no negotiations were possible until resistance had ceased. The generals and admirals appointed—General Gates, then General Howe and his brother Admiral Howe, General Clinton, then General Cornwallis—were never given authority to diverge from this position in a smallest particular. Granted the obstinacy and self-righteousness of George III and the immense financial and other resources of Great Britain, that meant a long war. Although, in 1775, British troops were thin on the ground, by summer 1776, the largest expeditionary force in British history—perhaps the largest ever dispatched from Europe until Napoleonic times—with thirty-two thousand fully equipped men was landed in the New York area.

This deployment was constantly reinforced, and was backed by half the world's largest and most efficient navy. George III could draw not only on his own troops but on mercenaries from Germany, and over thirty thousand of them (mainly Hessians) were sent across the Atlantic. With complete command of the sea until 1781, the British could land, embark, and land again their troops and artillery anywhere along the American seaboard, having safe fleet bases in Nova Scotia to the north and the West Indies and Bermuda to the south. In this sense they could dictate the strategy.

On the other hand, other than George III's obstinate resolve, they had no emotional commitment to the war. At the time of the first troubles in Massachusetts, 1773–74, there was some popular enthusiasm in England for the "rebels" to be "punished." But that soon disappeared, and thereafter the British public was indifferent. The war made virtually no impact on the letters, literature, and even newspapers of the time. The British were going through a revolution, not only in agriculture and industry but in transport, as the national system of canals and turnpikes was built. Money was being made in unprecedented quantities by most classes. British trade was expanding all over the world. At home, villages were expanding into towns, and their inhabitants changing their occupations, joining the wage economy. The people had other things on their minds. The crown was never short of a servile parliamentary majority of placemen and pocket-borough MPs to vote for the war, and economic expansion made it comparatively easy to pay for it. But few had any idea what was going on across the Atlantic, and fewer still cared.

It might have been different if George III and his ministers had been able to organize an effective loyalist party in America. Washington calculated that only one third of the people, chiefly in Massachusetts and Virginia, actually supported the war, and that a third were loyalists (the rest were uncommitted). But, by his own definition, George III could never treat the loyalists as allies—they, too, were merely "subjects." So there was no attempt to organize them, and no leaders appeared. The loyalists never posed a military threat to Washington, or a political threat to Congress. All leaders of opinion were on the Revolutionary side. In Britain it was the reverse: all the politicians of substance, the opinion-formers, the ministers, and such churchmen as carried weight thought the king mistaken and wanted a negotiated settlement. Washington was aware of these sentiments and knew that if he could hang on long enough, all support in Britain for the war would disappear. He also calculated, rightly, that the longer the inconclusive war continued, the more likely it was Britain's European enemies—French, Spanish, Dutch—whom she had robbed of their colonies, would join in against her, and indeed from the first years of the fighting, Benjamin Franklin was able to set about organizing arms supplies from France. A central element of Washington's strategy, and a source of his confidence, was that time was on his side.

Nevertheless, the burdens he carried were almost beyond even his energy and resourcefulness. The British initially believed their early victory was inevitable because militiamen and civilian soldiers could not stand up against regular troops. They were proved wrong;

yet Washington himself partly shared this belief. As he put it to one of his principal correspondents in Congress, John Hancock, September 24, 1776:

> To place any dependence upon Militia is assuredly, resting upon a broken staff. Men just dragged from the tender scenes of domestic life, unaccustomed to the din of arms: totally unacquainted with any kind of Military Skill, which being followed by a want of confidence in themselves, when opposed to Troops regularly trained, disciplined and appointed, superior in Knowledge and superior in Arms, makes them timid and ready to fly from their own shadows.

He found this true, time and again, and it was essential in his eyes for the bulk of his army to be on regular engagement. The difficulty was that, under the Articles of Association, 1775–76, precursor of the U.S. Constitution, Congress could not raise taxes to pay a national army: it could merely negotiate levies from individual states. Much of Washington's time, and two thirds of his vast wartime correspondence, was devoted to begging money and supplies from his political superiors—in this unremitting effort he was, happily, as obstinate as George III in continuing the war. Even so, as he wrote to Nathaniel Greene after it was all over in 1783: "It will not be believed that such a force as Great Britain has employed for eight years in this country could be baffled in their plan of subjugating it, by numbers infinitely less, composed of men oftentimes half starved, always in rags, without pay and experienced every species of distress, which human nature is capable of undergoing."

It was precisely because he appreciated the heroism of his troops, and sympathized with their sufferings, that he made every effort in his power to stiffen civilian backing for the war and prevent any truck with the enemy. An important letter to Lund Washington, in charge at Mount Vernon, has survived, in which he rebukes Lund for supplying a British naval sloop, anchored below the house, with food in return for a promise to leave the estate and its slaves alone. "That which gives me the worse concern," he wrote, "is that you should go aboard the enemy's vessel and furnish them with refreshments. It would have been a less painful circumstance to me to have heard that in consequence of your non-compliance with their request, they had burnt my house and laid the plantation in ruins."

This letter, undoubtedly sincere, illustrated the extent and depth of Washington's conviction. To sacrifice his own beloved home, he felt, was the least he could do, granted his inability to win a decisive battle with the tiny means at his disposal. He wrote: "We should on all occasions avoid a general action and never [be] drawn into a necessity to put anything to the risque . . . I am sensible a retreating army is incircled with difficulties; that declining an engagement subjects a general to reproach . . . but when the fate of America may be at stake on the issue . . . We should protract the war if possible."

Hence his first move, as commander in chief, was to liberate Boston, the original center of resistance. Thanks to Knox's cannon, and the British decision to evacuate Boston and concentrate their forces in New York, he was able to do this on March 17, 1776. He then marched his small army to New York, and had the Declaration of Independence, just passed by Congress, read to all units on July 9. But he had only nineteen thousand inexperienced Continentals, as his regulars were called, and state militiamen, facing thirty-two thousand British redcoats. Stage by stage, he was driven out, losing the Battle of Long Island, August 27, withdrawing from Brooklyn Heights three days later, losing at White Plains on October 28, and Fort Washington on November 16, with twenty-eight hundred of his men taken prisoner. The retreat was sporadic but unending, and he performed prodigies to keep his army together. But there were successes, too. On December 25, in one of the most dramatic moments of the war, he personally led twenty-four hundred men in a night crossing of the Delaware River, which was choked with ice floes, and the next day defeated the Hessian garrison at Trenton, taking nine hundred prisoners. A week later, he personally led an attack at Princeton, breaking up the British force. These two minor victories did wonders for American morale, both in the army and in Congress.

Describing the Revolutionary War is difficult because it had little discernible pattern. The British had the initiative almost throughout because of their larger forces and overwhelming naval arm. But, with frequent changes of command, their strategy lacked consistency. General Burgoyne was sent south from Canada in 1777 to seize the Hudson valley and cut off New England—the seat of the rebellion in their eyes—from the rest of the colonies. General Howe should have moved up the Hudson to meet Burgoyne. Instead he moved south to Philadelphia and Pennsylvania. He defeated Washington at Brandywine Creek in September and Germantown in October. But in the meantime Burgoyne had been forced to surrender at Saratoga to a force under General Horatio Gates. That in turn led to a crisis in the American camp, for some officers, contrasting Washington's failures with Gates's successes, conspired to make him the commander in chief. The plot, called the Conway Cabal after General Thomas Conway, a disgruntled Irish volunteer, was easily frustrated by Washington's magnanimity, based on his knowledge that the entire rank and file supported him.

The winter of 1777–78 was seen, at the time, as the nadir of American fortunes. In fact, Washington's strategy of attrition was beginning to work. On February 6, 1778, France recognized American independence and signed a treaty of alliance, pledging military and naval help if this treaty led to war between Britain and France, which it soon did. Indeed, as early as July 8 a French fleet, with four thousand soldiers, arrived in American waters. In Washington's clear order of priorities, anything which prevented George III from reinforcing his army and his fleet from dominating American waters, had to come first. But then and later he hated the idea of entanglements with foreign European powers. He had been brought up to dislike the French, a feeling reinforced by fighting them. With the outstanding exception of the Marquis de Lafayette, a young enthusiast who became an unofficial member of his "family," he did not welcome French volunteers or mercenaries, his forces finding them, like the Irish, unreliable, politically minded, and with agendas of their own. He opposed any American strategy which involved invading Canada and overthrowing British rule there. He was terrified of a French military reentry into Canada, which he knew would be inevitably followed by French schemes in the Mississippi valley. His early experience of working with the French in 1778—an abortive Franco-American attack on Newport, Rhode Island, in August—was discouraging and increased his distrust. In his heart, Washington believed he could work with the British once they had recovered their traditional sense of realism, and that, with their all-powerful navy, they would be natural and valuable allies of an infant American republic, until it became strong enough to defend itself against all comers.

In the meantime, America had to fight them off, and the war dragged on painfully through 1779 and 1780. In some ways it was an old-fashioned conflict. The British resumed the ancient custom of passing the icy months in winter quarters, a practice that in continental Europe had been obsolescent since the days of Wallenstein and Gustavus Adolphus. Washington was only too glad to follow suit, at Cambridge in 1775; Morristown, 1776; Valley Forge, 1777; Middlebrook, 1778; Morristown, again in 1779; New Windsor, 1780; Newburgh, 1781; and Rocky Hill, 1782. These respites in the fighting and marching enabled him to reequip and train his men, and to spend more time dealing with Congress, and gouging money and supplies out of it: he was always joined by Martha, from December 1775 onward. Indeed she spent two thirds of the eight-year war in or near Washington's camp, a source of endless comfort to him, and one suspects that, without her sustenance and encouragement, he might have found the strain of his command, with its endless frustrations and reverses, unendurable. Moreover, Martha was accompanied by many other ladies, and these daughters of the Revolution tended the wounded and sick, vastly improved the diet and accommodation of the army, and raised morale. Their presence was something the British lacked, and it told. We have pictures of Washington relaxing with his officers, playing handball and football, riding, hunting, and shooting.

The failure of the British to fight a continuous, all-weather war played directly into Washington's strategic hands. But American reverses continued. On May 12, 1780, Clinton attacked the south in great force, taking Charleston and over five thousand prisoners. He then returned to New York, the center of royalism, leaving Earl Cornwallis behind with eight thousand men, and in August he routed Horatio Gates at the Battle of Camden in South Carolina. Washington had other problems to contend with: the treachery of Benedict Arnold, which he discovered in September 1780 while inspecting the key Hudson River fortress of West Point, which Arnold had planned to surrender to the British, and two serious mutinies, both at the Morristown bases, in May 1780 and January 1781. There was a further mutiny of New Jersey men at Pompton later in January, and Washington suppressed it by force, summarily executing the two ringleaders by firing squad on January 27.

In the meantime, however, Washington had been devising a joint strategy with the French land commander Count Rochambeau. At their meeting on May 21 and 22 in Connecticut, they planned a joint attack on New York, the heart of the British occupation. They concentrated their forces accordingly but on August 14 news reached Washington that Admiral de Grasse, with the bulk of the French fleet, was heading for Chesapeake Bay. He instantly grasped a matchless opportunity "to strike the enemy in the most vulnerable quarter." Earlier that month, following orders from Clinton, Cornwallis had established a fortified base at Yorktown on Chesapeake Bay. This strategy made sense only if Britain retained absolute command of the sea. What Washington had been waiting for, and now saw was happening, was a temporary loss of that vital supremacy. He immediately ordered all available American and French troops south, taking the risk of conveying many of them by sea on French ships. For a few months there were more French warships in the western Atlantic than British ones. Indeed, on September 5, in the Battle of Chesapeake Capes, the French fleet drove off a relieving British squadron of inferior numbers, forcing it to return to New York. Cornwallis now found himself trapped, with ammunition short and no hope of a relieving fleet for months. On September 30 Washington invested Yorktown with 9,000 American and 7,500 French troops, and strong siege batteries plentifully supplied with shot. Cornwallis really had no alternative but to ask for terms, and two days later his 7,250 men surrendered. As even Lord North said, when he got the news in London: "This is the end." After all his defeats and retreats, Washington had won a decisive victory by seizing a strategic opportunity. It was a crowning moment, and meant peace at last, though it was a long time coming—the Peace of Paris, September 3, 1783.

Long before this, Washington, the triumphant general, was being drawn into the political dimension. He was desperately anxious to return to Mount Vernon which, in eight long years, he had only briefly (three days) visited on his way to Yorktown. He had already lost his beloved stepdaughter, Patsy. On November 5, 1781, his stepson John Parke Custis, or Jacky, who had been on his staff at Yorktown, died of "camp fever," leaving a widow and four young children—the two youngest were raised at Mount Vernon. Martha, his comforter in winter quarters, badly needed comforting herself.

Clearly in his many and anguished dealings with Congress, Washington had become aware of its glaring weaknesses. He had had a good war, the politicians a bad one. Franklin, to be sure, had played a valuable role in bringing France into the conflict. But the others had made little contribution. John Adams, while making snide remarks about Washington's generalship, had given him little help in paying and supplying the army. Jefferson had been equally feeble. Both had been infrequent attenders of Congress. There was no leading political figure the general felt he could trust. In the army, among the officers, this antipolitical feeling was very strong. There was talk of abolishing Congress, setting up a strong government, and making Washington its dictator-king—exactly the kind of thinking that led to Bonaparte's transformation into the Emperor Napoleon two decades later. A Colonel Lewis Nicola, an Irish Huguenot, who obviously did not know Washington well, and was just the kind of ideologically minded foreigner the general distrusted, was rash enough to put the suggestion to Washington in a letter, and received the devastating reply, worth quoting in full, for it tells us so much about the man, when thus roused to constitutional passion:

Sir—With a mixture of great surprise and astonishment I have read with attention the sentiments you have submitted to my perusal. Be assured, Sir, no occurrence in the course of the War, has given me more painful sensations than your information of there being such ideas existing in the Army as you have expressed, and I must view them with abhorrence and reprehend with severity. For the present, the communication of them will rest in my own bosom, unless some further agitation of the matter, shall make a disclosure necessary.

I am much at a loss to conceive what part of my conduct could have given encouragement to an address, which to me seems big with the greatest mischiefs that can befall my Country. If I am not deceived in the knowledge of myself, you could not have found a person to whom your schemes are more disagreeable; at the same time, in justice to my own feelings I must add, that no Man possesses a more sincere wish to see complete justice done to the Army than I do, and as far as all my powers and influence in a constitutional way extend, they shall be employed to the utmost of my abilities to effect it, should there be any occasion. Let me conjure you then, if you have any regard for your Country, concern for yourself or posterity, or respect for me, to banish these thoughts from

Your Mind, and never communicate, as from yourself, or any one else, a sentiment of the like Nature.

Washington thus rejected a crown far more emphatically than Cromwell did. He went much further. By March 1783 anonymous papers (in fact written by Major John Armstrong) were circulated at Newburgh, demanding from Congress a redress of the army's grievances, especially over pay. Here was the ghost of Cromwell's New Model Army, threatening the civil forces. Washington rightly suspected senior officers, such as General Horatio Gates, of being in sympathy with this potential military coup, and he feared that the officers were "wavering on a tremendous precipice" above "a gulph of Civil horror," threatening to "deluge our rising Empire in blood."

Accordingly he summoned a dramatic meeting of officers for March 15, and put everything on the line—his person, his reputation, his authority, digging deep into the affection he knew almost all had for him. Samuel Shaw, who was present, recorded:

On other occasions he had been supported by the exertions of an army; but in this he stood single and alone . . . he appeared not at the head of his troops but as it were in opposition to them; and for a dreadful moment the intent of the Army and its General seemed to be in competition. He spoke—every doubt was dispelled, and the tide of patriotism rolled again in its wonted course.

The occasion showed not only that Washington was a superb orator when roused but that he was also a cunning operator. He wrote the draft of his speech in his own hand, and in large letters, deliberately, for in reading it he made a dramatic point of taking out his new reading glasses. He took some time to focus with them, and said: "Gentlemen, you must pardon me. I have grown grey in your service, and now find myself growing blind." Some would find this corny. But it worked, and thereafter the appeal was to willing listeners. He then, turning to Congress, used what he termed "the Grand Convention of the Officers" to good effect in persuading Congress to meet all the army's legitimate demands, without mentioning his speech at all, or giving any indication of the bellicosity of some officers. He told Congress that the procedures of the army "not only confirm their claim to the justice, but will increase their title to the Gratitude of this Country." It was a masterly piece of selective reasoning, neatly turning a potential coup into an actual occasion of lawful and constitutional behavior. One is tempted to say it was Washington's finest hour.

The actual resignation of his command, having made peace between the civil and military powers of the new country—and, in an emotional ceremony, bidden farewell to his officers on December 4, 1783—took place in Annapolis, Maryland, on December 23, when he formally handed back to Congress his commission as commander in chief, which they had given him in June 1775. He said he would never again hold public office. He had his horse waiting at the door, and he took the road to Mount Vernon the next day.

No one who knew Washington well was surprised. Everyone else, in varying degrees, was astonished at this singular failure of the corruption of power to work. And, indeed, it was a rare moment in history. In London, George III questioned the American-born painter Benjamin West what Washington would do now he had won the war. "Oh," said West, "they say he will return to his farm." "If he does that," said the king, "he will be the greatest man in the world."

Chapter Five

Creating a Nation: Theory

B ACK IN MOUNT VERNON, Washington, now fifty-two, took stock of his personal state, and the state of the nation. His farm and lands were in many cases run down, after his eight-year absence. Their scattered nature made his personal supervision difficult. Not for the first time he reflected that America's first problem was the tyranny of distance. It was vast, and growing each year, and communications were not keeping up. Washington might be called the first secular American, secular because some of the preachers of the Great Awakening at the time of his childhood had visited all of the colonies, indeed it was their ignition of a common religion flame that first gave the thirteen territories a sense of nationhood. Religious arousal was the prelude to political and military arousal. But Washington had traveled wider than any nonpreacher. He knew much of the frontier: indeed, in 1758–69 he had defended seven hundred miles of it with only five hundred men. He was always on the move, an intense (but practical) curiosity being one of his strongest characteristics. When he attended the first Continental Congress in Philadelphia in 1774 he had visited more of America than any other delegate had: the great majority were outside their own homeland for the first time. He fought the war over nine of the thirteen states and got to know large parts of the country with painful intimacy but also with a glowing regard for their potential. He saw America increasingly in unitary terms and this vision was strengthened by further travels both before the constitutional convention and during his presidency, when he made two major sweeps through the country, north and south. His diaries show what chiefly interested him: the impact of distance on the economy, social life, and opportunity. Any steps to speed up travel were central to the country's future. He noted that stagecoaches ran three times a week from Norfolk, Virginia, up to Portsmouth, New Hampshire. But just to get from Richmond to Boston by stage might take twelve days. There was one good wagon road into the interior, but south of Virginia, roads, stages, and tracks were so bad that people preferred to travel by sea, a sure sign of a primitive transport economy.

America, following in Britain's footsteps but vastly improving on her record, has made fast, extensive, cheap, safe, and reliable travel the essence of her civic craftsmanship. Washington was the pioneer. He realized early that the tyranny of distance could be reduced by intelligent use of her tremendous rivers, having canoed some of the fiercest himself. As early as 1769 he tried to promote the use of lock canals to improve natural waterways like the Potomac and Ohio. The canal (linked to improved post roads) was the dynamic of the revolution in transport of the eighteenth century, just as steam was for the nineteenth, and the internal combustion engine, in cars and aircraft, was for the twentieth. Washington's diaries show that as soon as the war was over he turned again and again to canals. In September 1784 he traveled across the Alleghenies partly to inspect his western lands but also to plan canal routes (and roads) to link Ohio tributaries to the Potomac. He covered 680 miles, often sleeping in the open. His training as a surveyor gave him valuable insights into viable schemes. In May 1785 he convened and presided at a meeting at Mount Vernon with commissioners from Virginia and Maryland to resolve disputes about making the maximum use of common waterways. The house was now big enough to accommodate the meeting, and Washington presided over it so skillfully, saying little himself but encouraging the best-briefed to speak, that it led to demands for a national conference on interstate trade, a first step toward a constitutional convention to replace the outdated and hasty Articles. In May he became president of the Potomac Navigation Company, empowered with a joint charter from Maryland and Virginia to improve roads and build canals throughout the area. As always, Washington pushed for the rapid development of the area, emphasizing that improved transport to the whole Ohio valley was the surest way to bind the settlements there to the states, and encourage new ones. The intensity of Washington's efforts are reflected in a letter James Madison sent to Thomas Jefferson in Paris:

*The earnestness with which he expresses the undertaking is hardly
to be described, and shows that a mind like his, capable of great
views, and which has long been occupied by them, cannot bear a
vacancy, and surely he could not have chosen an occupation more
worthy of succeeding to that of establishing the political rights of his
country than the patronage of works for the extensive and lasting
improvement of its natural advantages; works which will double
the value of half the lands within the Commonwealth, will extend
its commerce and link its interests with those of the western states.*

Washington certainly hustled the procedures that brought the
Potomac plan into law, and then into active service. His only problem was Virginia's decision to donate its 10 percent statutory shares
to Washington himself, in recognition both of his wartime services
and his energy in pushing forward the plan. This caused the general
intense embarrassment, since he did not want to accept the shares,
which went against his code of separating public service from private
interest; on the other hand, he did not want to offend the Virginian
assembly. Eventually a compromise was reached: the shares were accepted but turned into an educational trust. The many anxious letters Washington wrote to friends about this tricky matter betray once
again what might almost be called his moral vanity—his over-
scrupulous desire that every action of his should be, and be seen to
be, beyond any possible criticism.

At the same time he was applying himself to agriculture, relish-
ing the fact that he could once more indulge in his deep admiration

for the good achievements of the English, the most advanced nation in stock and arable farming. Arthur Young, editor of the *Annals of Agriculture* and England's leading theoretical expert, wrote to him, and the general replied with enthusiasm, though characteristically deprecating his knowledge and skill: "Agriculture has ever been amongst the most favourite amusements of my life, though I never possessed much skill in the art, and nine years total inattention to it, has added nothing to a knowledge which is best understood in practice."

His various long letters to Young are full of information about American agriculture, mostly to its disadvantage—as he put it, "An English farmer must entertain a contemptible opinion of our husbandry, or a horrid idea of our lands," when comparing output per acre. Washington made full use of Young's publications, and took steps to obtain their widest dissemination in the United States, and put their author in touch with progressive farmers. He also imported an English farm manager, seeds, plants, and equipment, and a Spanish jackass he used to breed mules. At this time he had at Mount Vernon 30 horses, 283 sheep, and 336 cattle, plus a large but unknown number of hogs, which ran wild. He also had 322 slaves but only a third worked, the rest being old, sick, or juvenile. He again declared his determination to end slavery, and belief that it could be done. "It is," he wrote, "among my first wishes to see some plan adopted by which slavery in this country may be abolished by slow, sure and imperceptible degrees." Its degradation and persistence were only one of his worries. Since his return from war, and his enlarged grasp of

American potential, he had been depressed by the weakness and inertia of Congress, and its inability to offer leadership given its feeble powers. His wartime concerns as a general were now transformed to his civil anxieties as a progressive economist and a practitioner of both food raising and manufacture (he milled flour, made bricks, and worked in other fields to produce goods for sale). He was nagged by the fear that state rivalries, such as that between Maryland and Virginia over river power, would destroy the young and fragile republic unless the federal, or general government as he called it (with a distinct military overtone), was strong enough to arbitrate. Hence the significance of the Potomac conferences and schemes he promoted was much wider than the water issue.

From September 11 to 14, 1786, the Annapolis Convention met to follow up the Potomac Conference by making wider agreements on interstate trade. At Washington's urging it passed a resolution calling for representatives from all states to meet in Philadelphia on May 14, 1787, "to desire such further provisions as shall appear to them necessary to render the constitution of the Federal Government adequate to the exigences of the Union." The move was given urgency by an event that caused Washington grave concern, the outbreak of Shays' Rebellion. Daniel Shays was a bankrupt Massachusetts farmer and former captain in Washington's army. In the autumn of 1786 he led an antitax revolt of similar poor farmers being prosecuted for nonpayment. They gathered at Springfield, where the state supreme court met, and forced it to adjourn in terror. In January Shays led twelve hundred men armed with pitchforks and primitive hunting guns toward the Springfield arsenal, to steal muskets and seize cannon. They were eventually scattered but some were still being hunted in February 1787, shortly before the Convention met. Some of Shays' statements about his destructive intentions were hair raising, and nothing could be more likely to persuade Washington that a stronger central government was needed now. Most constitutionalists of his day were influenced by John Locke but he, thanks to Alexander Hamilton, had also read key passages from Hobbes's *Leviathan*, stressing the anarchic behavior of humanity in its natural state and the need of an artificial constitutional giant figure "to keep them all in awe." Shays, to him, was the personification of lawless anarchy, and the decision of Massachusetts to drop direct taxation in response to his violence proved that governments would always be cowardly without Leviathan. Taxation, to pay regular, armed, and disciplined men to enforce order, was the fundamental principle of Washington's idea of government.

Hence, after his usual demurrers—the general always backed into the limelight—he agreed to attend the Convention, arrived in Philadelphia on May 13, 1787 (in civilian attire), and, as soon as a quorum was reached on May 23, was elected its president. He was the obvious and correct choice and chaired the meetings superbly, and his election helps to explain why the Convention got things to work so swiftly—it adopted the Constitution by vote on September 15, signed it two days later, and then dispersed. As presiding officer, Washington had the advantage that he was not expected to take part in debates. In fact he intervened only once, to help reduce the basic unit of population for representation from forty thousand to thirty thousand, and he did this solely in order to ensure agreement. He was able to take an irenic part throughout, combining patience, firmness, and benignity, inviting all to display commonsense behavior and brevity of speech to win his approval. His own attitude was studied moderation, what we would now call laid back. To emphasize this quality, he used the recess, July 26 to August 6, to go fishing, visit his old campsite at Valley Forge, pose for his portrait, and visit William Batram's botanical garden and the painter Charles Willson Peale's museum.

But the fact that he presided impartially does not mean he had no views or failed to forward them behind the scenes. Indeed, most delegates, knowing that Washington would be their first national leader, were only too anxious to tailor him a garment that would fit, and that he would wear comfortably. As the South Carolina delegate Pierce Butler wrote: "Many of the members cast their eyes toward General Washington as President; and shaped their Ideas of the powers to be given to a President, by their Opinion of his Virtue." What he wanted was the widest possible agreement on the Constitution, ensuring that it would secure the widest possible obedience once enacted; and, secondly, wide discretionary powers for the chief executor (and the executors as a whole) in the event of unforeseen difficulties. This was the rational view of an experienced wartime commander who had no love of power for its own sake but saw it as a disagreeable necessity at times. And this rational view permeated the Convention.

Washington also had two unacknowledged agents working for him. James Madison had already devised and largely written Virginia's own constitution, much to the general's approval. His experience and skills he now brought to the larger constitutional enterprise, which was mainly his doing. Washington backed this, too, as the Constitution was the most likely document to secure general approval at the Convention and subsequent ratification by the nation (or "the Publick," as he liked to call it). Second, any danger the Constitution might err too largely in favor of states' powers and produce a weak federal government—for Madison was much under the influence of Jefferson, an antifederalist—was redressed by the active participation of Alexander Hamilton. Then, as in the war, he was the statesman-commander closest to Washington, most often in private consultation with him, and whose views were respected not only because of his brilliant military career, legal expertise, and sheer knowledge of a vast range of subjects, but because it was known he had the general's ear.

The Constitution as a whole, to Washington's approval, adopted Madison's outline, what was known as the Virginia plan. But it also, and again with the general's approval, adopted two important compromises, both with the net result of favoring a strong federal system. The first, the Connecticut Compromise, embodied Washington's wartime experience that Congress must be able to tax freely and take key military and foreign policy decisions without always looking over its shoulder at the states. So the federal legislature was composed as follows: the House of Representatives, directly elected by popular vote in the localities, was given control of money, and a Senate, particularly charged with foreign affairs, was there to uphold states' interests, with two members for each state, irrespective of population or territory, and originally chosen by state legislatures. The second Compromise, which came early in September, and crowned the edifice, involved the presidency. Hamilton (it is too early yet to say Washington, too) lost the battle for a centralized state, which remained decentralized rather than concentrated) but he (and certainly Washington, too) won a significant victory over the way in which a president was to be chosen and the powers he would exercise. By skillful compromise, Hamilton got the president elected not by Congress or the state legislators but by a quite separate electoral college, which was heavily dependent (and of course increasingly so as time went by) on popular participation. In time this meant that the president was the only official to be directly chosen by the entire nation, with all the moral authority the election gave. His powers, too, were potentially enormous. He had the right of veto (offset by a two-thirds overriding rule) over congressional legislation, and extremely wide executive powers (partially offset by an "advice and consent" power vested in the Senate). Almost by accident America got a strong presidency, or rather an office that any particular president could make strong in accordance with the needs of the times. He was much stronger than most kings of the day, rivaled or exceeded only by the "Great Autocrat," the czar of Russia (and in practice stronger than most czars); almost as strong, in emergency, as Napoleon Bonaparte in the next generation, because Bonaparte was only as strong, in practice, as his last military victory made him. These powers, still buried in the thickets of constitutional ambiguity, were exercised as American history progressed, during the nineteenth century, first by Andrew Jackson, then by Abraham Lincoln. They were only conferred in the first place because the delegates knew they would be shaped in practice by the wise and moderate man who presided over them, and who had long since demonstrated that he, for one, could not be corrupted by office into the love of power. The American Constitution was the work of an oligarchy of able men, the Founding Fathers. But there is a case for arguing that the most influential of them all was Washington, not by his voice but by his public silence, his presence, and his record of republican virtue and decisive action speaking louder than words.

The ratification process was almost as important as the business of drawing up the document. That was one reason Washington was so anxious to ensure, by compromise, that the ratification would succeed. Article VII of the Constitution set it out, in four stages—approval by the old Congress of the Confederates; presentation to the individual states; election of delegates in each state to consider it; and, finally, ratification by these state delegates in at least nine of the thirteen states. Once the ninth state signaled acceptance, the Constitution became law. The securing of a majority rule instead of unanimity was an important victory for the federalists—and for Washington, who watched over the four-stage process with anxiety and growing confidence. He thought that the four biggest states, New York, Pennsylvania, Virginia, and Massachusetts, would ratify and, in effect, clinch the issue. He also believed the people wanted a decision and this is why he supported ratification by directly elected delegates. He was right on both fronts, and also on the drift of the great public debate that preceded the ratification votes. He took no part whatever in the debate, being careful to keep his views to himself, except in a few private letters. But his views were known or guessed, and the public responded. The debate was in splendid spoken words and resounding print. America got its first proper daily newspaper in 1783, the *Philadelphia Evening Post* and by the late 1780s, dailies and weeklies were proliferating. Washington himself took ten, regularly, and read them over breakfast. He also bought, read, and kept numerous pamphlets. But, while following the debates with the closest attention from Mount Vernon, he did not intervene. He wanted ratification but he was "well disposed to let the matter rest entirely on its own merits, and men's minds to their own workings." New York ratified in July 1788, making eleven states and ensuring adoption. By the summer, then, his mind was at rest: the new nation was to have a proper government, generally approved. His only worry was that he would be called upon to work it. But this was now inevitable, and he had, in his own mind, accepted the duty long before the presidential electors met on February 4, 1789, and voted unanimously for him. Now came the last great test of his life.

Chapter Six

Creating a Nation: Practice

ASHINGTON WAS OFFICIALLY notified he was the president when the first federal Congress reached its quorum on April 6, 1789, and he immediately hurried to New York, the temporary capital. To cover his immediate debts and his travel expenses, he borrowed £600. Nevertheless, having sworn the oath of office at Federal Hall on April 30, he initially declined a salary. But Congress would not have it. They expected to be paid. So did senior members of the administration now formed. Vice President John Adams, elected by a vote of thirty-four, demanded a salary; so did Alexander Hamilton, Treasury secretary, who was rich and did not need the money but who spoke for the lawyers who were adamant for pay in all public offices, and who constituted the biggest single element in the administration. Jefferson, secretary of state, would have sided with Washington, on principle, but being deeply in debt was relieved when the president gave way and accepted twenty-five thousand dollars a year.

How he or anyone else was to be paid regularly was a moot question, for the federal government was bankrupt and its currency worthless. His first act was to commission Hamilton, a financial wizard who had been discussing the problem with other New York experts since the early years of the decade, to put the national finances on a sound footing at any cost. The situation was this. In 1775 Congress authorized an issue of $2 million in bills of credit called Continentals to finance the war. By the end of 1779, $241.6 million had been issued and this was only part of the borrowing, which included foreign loans, state loans, U.S. Loan Certificates, and other paper and produced the worst inflation in U.S. history. By 1780 the Continentals were in practice valueless. In 1782 Congress reckoned that its debts in hard money were $27 million but it had to go on issuing more paper to pay interest because it was not authorized by law to tax. By early 1790, despite some help from the states, the federal government's debts were $40 million domestic and $13.2 million foreign. Its paper fetched only 15 to 30 cents on the dollar. This was precisely the kind of disaster that was to hit all the new Latin American governments in the next generation, and from which some have never recovered; and it was the common fate of the new states that came into existence in the twentieth century. But Washington and Hamilton agreed that the United States, which sprang from the stock of England, whose credit was the model for the world, must follow the mother country.

By January 1790 Hamilton had produced his "Report on the Public Credit" for Congress. This gave holders of Continentals one dollar for every hundred paper, which they grumblingly accepted, it being better than nothing. All the rest of the debt was funded and rescheduled as long-term securities payable in gold. The government also assumed the war debts of the states, on the same terms. This was attacked as unfair, since some states had already paid their debts, and the arrangement favored the reckless at the expense of the provident. But Hamilton, with the president's full backing, was adamant: the all-important object was to get rid of the debt once and for all, and start the country afresh on a sound basis of credit and hard money. The plan was expensive? So be it: America was potentially an enormously rich country—richer than Britain, per capita, and getting finance right was the quickest way to realize that wealth, not least by earning the right to borrow cheaply on world markets. The plan benefited the rich, who held paper money? Of course. Hamilton knew—though he did not say so—that two thousand years of history proved that state financial proposals that do not benefit the rich to some extent are most unlikely to prosper. Helped by a curious bargain proposed by Jefferson, under which in return for voting for the Report, the new federal capital was to be placed on the Potomac, instead of farther north, Hamilton got his way and was soon proved right. By 1791, when the plan came into action, federal per capita debt was $197 million (adjusted to modern dollars), a figure it was not to reach again until the Civil War. By 1804 it had fallen to $120 million and by 1811 to $49 million. As a result, when America wanted to borrow

$11.25 million in 1803 to finance the Louisiana Purchase—the greatest territorial bargain in history—it had no trouble raising the money at easy rates. In the meantime, Washington was able to run the government without the crushing burden of an insoluble debt problem overshadowing every move he made. It is impossible to exaggerate the debt every American owes to Hamilton for devising this bold scheme, and to Washington for giving him such firm backing that Congress had to carry it out.

Washington ran his administration on a nonparty basis. He hated party, and as head of state as well as government had to be above it. And he was above it in the sense that he did not fit into the stereotypes of either of the two groups now forming—the federalists, led by Hamilton, who wanted a strong centralized government on the English-European model, or the supporters of Jefferson, favoring decentralization and power vested firmly in the states. Events and practical necessities tended to push the president in a federalist direction, but many of his interests were those of a Virginian landowner, and so Jeffersonian. His aim, however, was to run them both in harness, indeed to run the cabinet as a body that represented regions, more than parties. But there was no disguising the fact that, after the president himself, Hamilton was the most powerful man in the country. This was resented by Jefferson who, as secretary of state, was the senior, in theory. But Hamilton, with Washington's full and active support, had clout. At this point, the Treasury ran everything not specifically allotted to other departments. For instance, it controlled the Post Office, which employed 325 people, more than half the entire federal bureaucracy. Hamilton was always expanding his empire. In addition to compiling his report on debt, he was asked by Washington (and Congress) to compile two more. One was on a national bank, which Hamilton expanded into the Bank of the United States, rather like the Bank of England. Washington did not understand banking but knew from bitter experience that a true banking system was much needed in the United States and that one was unlikely to come into existence without federal help. He liked the Bank of England and had held its gilt-edged Consols for many years, getting his quarterly interest on the dot and seeing his capital rise in terms of U.S. values. But Jefferson saw the bank as another symbol of centralist tyranny.

Jefferson was still more opposed to Hamilton's report recommending some federal assistance to U.S. manufacturers. Jefferson believed, as Washington had once done in theory, in an America on Roman lines, with wealth created by landowners and farmers. But Washington had discovered, when running the army, how vital local manufacturing was to supply musket and cannon, ammunitions and uniforms. In any case, he shared Hamilton's realistic view that it was all too late to build a Roman America: the industrial age was already taking over. Many of Washington's dearest schemes to expand and accelerate transport demanded workshops and factories, roads and bridges, turnpikes and canals. He had already met John Fitch and discussed with him his plans to speed up canal traffic by new kinds of propulsion, including (from 1789) steam. In 1787 and 1788 the first two big textile factories, in cotton and wool, opened in New England. So, with all due misgivings, the president backed Hamilton's policy, and it was during his presidency that America achieved takeoff into self-sustaining industrial growth.

It has to be understood, then, that for a time at least Washington's cabinet contained its own opposition to the dominant federalist tendency. His patience, magnanimity, and broadmindedness made this possible. Contemporary opinion varied on how well he ran the cabinet. The term itself did not actually come into use until 1793, but regular meetings with Jefferson, Hamilton, Knox, and Attorney General Randolph began to take place from early 1791, with the object of discussing policies and, in particular, whether presidential decisions and legislation (such as the Bank Act) were constitutional or not—a point on which Washington was always anxious to be reassured by colleagues. This was one reason he was keen to have men of varying political opinion within his inner circle. John Adams, vice president, and busy with the Senate, was not usually invited to such gatherings, one reason why he was so critical of his chief. Jealous and acerbic, he called Washington Old Muttonhead. He said he was primarily an actor, playing a role running the state that he did not fully grasp. "But we [in the Administration] all agreed to believe him and make the world believe him." He added that all Washington's apparent profundity came from Rollin's *Ancient History*—"but I will take my deepest secrets to the grave." Timothy Pickering, by then postmaster-general, war secretary, and secretary of state, was far more critical. He said Washington often dozed off in cabinet, never read dispatches, wrote few if any of his own speeches, and needed chalk marks on the floor to tell him where to stand at receptions. In general he was an illiterate and incompetent cipher propped up by his staff. But these charges by a savage and bad-tempered man are contradicted by so much other evidence as to be hardly worth repeating: Washington was particularly meticulous at getting through his paperwork, for instance.

It is true he was a bit of an actor. He liked to play the Old Man card when needed. He did his little scenes, as when addressing his officers at Newburgh, of fumbling for his glasses and repeating: "I have already grown grey in the service of my country—now I am growing blind." He also pretended to lose his temper. Jefferson, who was taken in, said he was "tremendous in his wrath." If ever his integrity was impugned in cabinet he would "By God Them," saying "he would rather be on his farm than be made Emperor of the World, by God!" He never pulled rank or boasted but by an occasional aside he would remind colleagues that he had won the war, almost singlehanded at times, whereas none of them, with the notable exceptions of Hamilton and Knox (both his protégés) had done nothing in arms. Jefferson fairly observed: "His heart was warm in its affections but he exactly calculated every man's value and gave him a solid esteem proportional to it."

In New York, as president, Washington lived in a seemly but not grandiose style. His household was small, only fourteen—smaller than at Mount Vernon—and his working secretariat tiny. His workload was heavy. He sometimes chose to give the impression (as did later successful presidents, such as Coolidge, Eisenhower, and

Reagan) that he was idler than he was. Much key business was dispatched between dawn and breakfast, with no one around. Jefferson said he set up a lot of ceremonial occasions to avoid too close contact with the people, whom he distrusted; he accused the president of sitting on a sofa placed on a dais. (This last point was hearsay and untrue.) In fact Washington shrewdly judged that most people wanted a bit of ceremony from their head of state, something Ronald Reagan rediscovered when, after the demotics of the Ford and Carter presidencies, he restored the grand manner protocol at the White House. It is true that Washington's formal dinners tended to be long and dull, with many slow courses. Senator Maclay, sharp tongued like Adams and Pickering, recalled: "No cheering ray of convivial sunshine broke through the cloudy gloom of settled seriousness. At every interval of eating or drinking, he played on the table with a knife and fork, like drumsticks." (But then Maclay had a bad word for all: Madison was "His Littleness," Adams "a monkey just put into breeches," Governeur Morris was "half envoy, half pimp.") The fact that Washington tried to avoid the universal handshake, bowing instead in the old English manner, was held against him by some. But it was his manner, which went with a courtesy already becoming rare. And a shake from the president's enormous and powerful paw could be bone grinding, so the frailer visitor, especially ladies, preferred a stately bow.

Jefferson's claim that Washington wished to put up protocol barriers between himself and the people is belied by his earnest attempt to meet as many as possible, not in a drawing-room in New York, but in their own districts. None of his immediate successors made any attempt to see the country: Washington's two great tours were major events to the hundreds of thousands of citizens who saw him—many of whom insisted on shaking hands and offering him a "ceegar"—the only chance in their lives of glimpsing a live president. And what a sight for families whose humdrum lives lacked color! The president had a white coach, secondhand but rebuilt by Clarke Brothers of Philadelphia for $950. The coachman was German, Tom Fagan, tall and strong, sitting on a leopardskin-covered box, alongside Major Jackson, the president's aide-de-camp. Also aboard were the valet, two footmen, and a mounted postillion riding behind. There was a light wagon for baggage, and five saddle horses including the famous charger Prescott, white and sixteen hands high, who had fought in seven of the president's battles and was the equivalent of the Duke of Wellington's Copenhagen or Napoleon's Marengo. Tremendous blasts of trumpet and bugle announced the arrival of the coach in any locality, and all rushed out to see the man who had won their freedom and was now visiting them according to republican law. He took these journeys out of curiosity and to gain useful knowledge but also because he knew "the Publick" wanted to see him. His travels were periodically highly uncomfortable and sometimes dangerous. He was nearly drowned crossing the Severn near Baltimore on a ferry. "I was in imminent danger from the unskilfulness of the hands and the dullnes of her sailing," he noted. The white coach and all aboard plunged into the foaming waters of the Occoquan Creek. Moving through rural America in the 1790s it was impossible for anyone, however important, to keep his ceremonial dignity. But Washington managed to retain the respect of all, even while traveling rough or listening to fifteen verbose toasts, plus speeches, at a tedious parish dinner in Maryland. Tobias Lear, who kept his records, noted he was "almost the only man of an exalted character who does not lose some part of his respectability on an intimate acquaintance." He cursed but he never grumbled. He By Godded them, but he also laughed when harnesses snapped or mud splashed through the open carriage window.

The president, often on the move, was a man of action when required. In 1791 Hamilton insisted that, to fund the debt and pay the expenses of the federal government, Congress must impose an excise tax, chiefly on whiskey (this in addition to his 1789 import tariff of 8 percent). Some frontiersmen, who made whiskey and regarded it as their only currency—they rarely earned or handled cash—saw this duty as a threat to their existence. Many felt that their incessant war with Indians, on behalf of all, was a form of civic service which should exempt them from tax. These men were self-righteous and aggressive—and armed. To them, the Excise Act was as wicked as the Stamp Act their fathers had rejected. Nonpayment became habitual. In July 1794 federal law officers tried to summon sixty notorious tax evaders before the court in Philadelphia. This led to an armed riot in which a U.S. soldier was killed and the head tax collector's home was burned. Moreover, despite a direct request from Hamilton, Governor Mifflin of Pennsylvania refused to send in the militia.

In Washington's view, this was treason-rebellion, and he authorized Hamilton to conscript fifteen thousand militiamen from Maryland, Virginia, and New Jersey, as well as Pennsylvania, and send them in under General Henry Lee. So there marched across the Alleghenies a larger force than any Washington had ever directly commanded, Hamilton with personal orders to do the thing thoroughly from the president and commander in chief, who was quite ready to take the field in person. The insurgents melted away and Jefferson scoffed that it was "the Rebellion that could never be found." Two ringleaders were convicted but Washington spared them hanging: in his view, an important point had been made, and it was never necessary, in his lifetime or for long after, for internal defiance of the constitutional law to be put down by federal force.

It was, indeed, one of Washington's achievements that he gave America a federal government that was able to act decisively when required, this being implicit in the presidential powers. Many of his successors have felt reason to be grateful to him. At the same time, America needed a constitution to ensure liberty, and most states, in agreeing to ratify it as it stood, added a rider that one of the first tasks of the new federal Congress must be to enact a Bill of Rights to safeguard the freedom of the individual in accordance with the Declaration of Independence. Washington was anxious to proceed swiftly on the rights issue, and once again, as with the Constitution itself, he was able to rely heavily on Madison, who had as precedent the Virginia Declaration of Rights (1776), actually drawn up by George Mason, a man whom Washington much admired for his sagacity.

Early in the presidency, Madison produced drafts of ten amendments to the Constitution. The first, the most important, prohibits legislative action in key areas, giving citizens freedom of religion, assembly, speech, press, and petitioning. The next seven protect property and the rights of defendants, and the ninth all rights not specifically enumerated. The tenth sums up: "The powers not delegated to the United States by the Constitution, not prohibited by it to the States, are reserved to the States respectively, or to the people." The passage of the bill, which Washington was known to favor, proceeded rapidly and on December 15, 1791, when a ratifying quorum was reached, became law.

Its most important element concerns religion. As Washington wished, religion figures only briefly in the Constitution itself. But the First Amendment, again with his sanction, specifically rejects a national church and forbids Congress to make "any law respecting an establishment of religion or prohibiting the free exercise thereof." This prohibition has been widely misunderstood in our own times and interpreted as a constitutional veto over anything religious taking place with federal approval or on federal property. In fact it was nothing of the sort. Such an interpretation would have angered Washington, who saw the provision as aimed at any attempt to erect a national church of any denomination. He detested the feeble and ambiguous form of Protestantism represented by the Church of England, and the bigoted versions of New England. He was by instinct a Deist rather than a Christian. But he would have been incensed to have been called a non-Christian, let alone an anti-

Christian. All his codes of morals, order, and propriety were rooted in Christianity, which he saw as the greatest civilizing force the world had ever known. He was a man of exceptional tolerance, and wrote of immigrants, whom he did not much esteem as a rule: "If they are good workmen, they may be of Asia, Africa or Europe. They may be Mohamedans, Jews or Christians of any sect, or they may be atheists." But such new arrivals had to recognize that they were joining a community under God—or Providence or "the Great Ruler of Events," to use favorite expressions of his—and the paramount mode of worship of this God was Christian. The notion that the First Amendment would be twisted into an instrument to prohibit the traditional practices of Christianity would have horrified him. He served for many years as a vestryman of his local Anglican-style church because he believed this to be a pointed gesture of solidarity with an institution he regarded as underpinning a civilized society. An America without religion as the strongest voluntary source of morality was to him an impossibility.

It is significant that the day after the House of Representatives passed the First Amendment, on September 25, 1789, it also passed, by a two-to-one majority, a resolution calling for a day of national prayer and thanksgiving, and asked Washington to appoint the day. The Resolution reads: "We acknowledge with grateful hearts the many signal favours of Almighty God, especially by affording them an opportunity peacefully to establish a constitutional government for their safety and happiness." Appointing the national holiday of Thanksgiving, Washington replied, in words equally significant: "It is the duty of all nations to acknowledge the providence of Almighty God, to obey His Will, to be grateful for His mercy, to implore His protection and favour . . . That great and glorious Being who is the beneficent author of all the good that was, that is, or that ever will be, that we may then unite in rendering unto Him an sincere and humble thanks for His kind care and protection of the people."

Where Washington failed over the Bill of Rights was to make provision for slaves to be liberated. In 1786 he vowed never to purchase another slave, and he expressed the wish that slavery throughout America be "abolished by slow, sure and imperceptible degrees." He may have regretted that, in the debates over the Constitution, which he chaired in silence, he never let his views on slavery be known. His friend George Mason, who owned more slaves than Washington, attacked the institution and especially the slave trade. Indeed, Article 1, Section 9, grants Congress the power to regulate or ban the slave trade as of January 1, 1808. But Washington was aware that there was no prospect of the South ratifying a constitution that did not recognize (and by implication legitimize) slavery in some way. The Constitutional Convention did so in three ways. It omitted any condemnation. It adopted Madison's three-fifths rule, which gave the slave states the added power of counting slaves as voters on the basis that each was three-fifths of a freeman, while of course denying them the vote as such. Thirdly, the words "slave" and "slavery" were deliberately avoided in the text. These concessions to slaveowners were necessary to get the text through at all, and Washington judged it more important to get a good constitution enacted and ratified than to do something dramatic about slavery. What he hoped, and kept on hoping, was that, as president, he might be able to do something himself. But in the end all he managed was to free his own slaves in his will (and even this only after his wife's death). All the same, that was regarded at the time as a remarkable gesture from a Virginia gentleman. The tragedy is that, in the late 1780s or early 1790s, it was still possible to set emancipation in steady motion without a civil war. After the 1790s, the growth of King Cotton made it impossible. So a chance was missed to save the America of the future a vast burden of misery, and it was on Washington's watch that the opportunity was lost. That, it can be agreed, was his one great failure.

He was much less sensitive on the subject of Indians. He referred to them as "savages." One of his complaints about them was that they ill treated their black slaves. The Treaty of Paris had left many unresolved matters, especially on the ground. The British still occupied forts in the Northwest Territory they had promised to evacuate in 1783, and Washington suspected that their agents kept the Indians of the region in a state of hostility toward American settlers. He dreaded the idea of going to war with the British again. He consistently refused to make claims over Canada and he would certainly have avoided the mistakes of Jefferson and Madison, which led in the next century to the lamentable War of 1812. But he was adamant that rebellious Indians must be put down with such severity as he was prepared to use against tax rebels. In 1791 he sent a large expedition under General Arthur St. Clair against the Northwest Indians and took particular trouble to caution him against being taken by surprise. On November 4 that is precisely what happened, and St. Clair suffered more than nine hundred casualties. The president was wrathful and replaced him by General Anthony Wayne, who did rather better. As the president put it, he "damped the ardor of the savages, and weakened their obstinacy" in waging war against the United States. However, as his original instructions to St. Clair in October 1791 show, he was worried about whether he was entering a "just" war or not, and he later insisted to Congress that America must be willing "to cement a lasting peace, upon terms of candor, equity and good neighbourhood." He emphasized: "Towards none of the Indian tribes have overtures of friendship been spared."

His relations with Congress, especially during his first term, began cordially and remained cordial. There was one notable exception. Early in his first term, August 22–24, 1789, he agreed to appear in person before the Senate to seek its "advice and consent" on a treaty with the Creek Indians. In June he had suffered a painful carbuncle on his left leg and had it lanced, but it recovered only slowly. That may have made him irascible. At all events he resented the tone of senatorial questioning and swore he would never appear before Congress again, a wise decision respected by all of his successors. He was not afraid of using his veto, either. On April 5, 1792, he "disapproved" a bill appointing electors. He believed the veto should apply only to bills he judged unconstitutional, and this was the reason; Congress, without fuss, upheld the veto.

By this point Washington was talking of a final return to Mount

Vernon. He prepared to draft a farewell address and on May 20, 1792, asked Madison to polish it. He was upset by the growing antagonism between Hamilton and Jefferson, reflected in cabinet wrangles. He saw, rightly, that two parties—the Federalists and the future Democrats (then, confusingly, calling themselves Republicans or Republican Democrats)—were emerging, and a personal effort he made to reconcile Jefferson and Hamilton did not work. He was also beginning to resent the critical tone of the press—and wondered why he should put up with insinuations against his honor. But all his principal colleagues urged him to run again, arguing that, for the present at least, he was indispensable. Their views would not have been decisive. He was talked into continuing by the ladies. Like many strongly masculine men of action—Wellington is another example—Washington preferred feminine to masculine company. With a lady at his side, there was no using the cutlery like drumsticks at dinner time. He preferred them even to clever, ingenious young men like Hamilton. One lady who particularly favored a second term was Eliza Powell, wife of Sam Powell, former mayor of Philadelphia. She was a leading hostess in her home city. In 1790 the government, as agreed, moved from New York to Philadelphia, to remain until the new federal capital on the Potomac was ready (Washington had already chosen the ten-mile site, to be named after him). That would not be until the 1800s, and Mrs. Powell looked forward to having Washington as her lion for the whole of his second term—the first instance in American history of a hostess influencing events. Then there was Henrietta Liston, enchanting wife of the British envoy

Robert Liston. She took the view (held now by the entire London establishment) that Washington was the best possible president, in British as well as American interests. He was a "sensible man" (Jane Austen's favorite term of praise) with "good feelings" as well as "bottom" (strength of character), who added "respectability" to America as a negotiating partner and future friend.

Most likely Washington made up his mind himself, believing that the international skies were darkening and that America needed a steady, moderate, and experienced captain on the ship of state. He withdrew his threats of going in the summer of 1792, and on December 2 received all the votes of the 132-member electoral college. Adams, with seventy-seven votes, remained vice president. Events soon confirmed Washington's view that foreign affairs would dominate his second term. Inaugurated on March 4, 1793, he received next month the news that France had declared war on Britain. Jefferson immediately pointed out that America had a 1778 Treaty of Alliance with France. He promptly had a row in cabinet with Hamilton, who favored neutrality with a benevolent inclination to Britain. The president insisted on a declaration of neutrality, an important first instance of the presidential power to determine foreign policy, if necessary and prudent, without consulting Congress. Neutrality, he insisted again and again in this second term, was "in America's *interests,* which she must follow while reserving all her rights." He felt it incumbent on him, as the first president, to stress the Americanism of her policy: she was not yet another European nation, obliged to make choices of allies and combinations but a completely new transatlantic entity making her own decisions according to rules of self-interest that had nothing necessarily to do with Old Europe. Washington, as president, was the first proponent of American exceptionalism. As he had put it to Patrick Henry: "In a word I want an *American* character, that the powers of Europe may be convinced we act for *ourselves* and not for others." To Pickering he insisted: "We must never forget that we are *Americans,* the remembrance of which will convince us we act for *ourselves* and not for *others.*" As he was soon to say in his Farewell Address: "The name of American which belongs to you, in your natural capacity, must always exalt the just pride of nationalism."

He was confirmed in this view by the gruesome events in France: the bloodbaths in the provinces, the execution of the king, then the queen, the terror, the successive *réglements des comptes,* as the revolutionary Saturns devoured their children. He deplored the formation of "Democratic Societies" of pro-French radicals, to which Jefferson gave his countenance, and was horrified by the arrival, as French envoy, of an excitable *enragé,* Edmond Charles Genêt, as part of Revolutionary France's policy "war with all Kings and peace with all peoples" (decree of November 19, 1792). Genêt arrived in Philadelphia on the frigate *L'Ambuscade* (a name Washington detested), which saluted him with a broadside against all protocol. Even before he had presented his credentials, he summoned the Americans to "erect the *Temple of Liberty* on the ruins of *palaces and thrones.*" This outraged Washington's feelings, since he had spent eight years fighting and winning a war that had erected a temple of liberty of America's own, leaving no palaces and thrones left to ruin. Meanwhile, Genêt made his propaganda headquarters at Philip Freneau's newspaper the *National Gazette*, 209 Market Street, Philadelphia, almost in earshot of Washington's house. Nothing could have been more calculated to turn the president against France. Freneau had been brought to town to run what was regarded as *the* opposition newspaper as a result of what has been called the first political party convention in American history. This took place before the second election on a so-called "botanizing expedition" up the Hudson, featuring Jefferson, Madison, George Clinton of New York, and Aaron Burr, future boss of the Tammany machine, who was later to murder Hamilton in a duel. Genêt used Freneau's paper to publicize his intentions to transform American politics—"I excite the *Canadiens* to break their British yoke. I am the *Kentukois* and propose a naval expedition which will facilitate their descent upon New Orleans." He denounced Washington's lack of enthusiasm for the cause and said he would "appeal from the president to the people."

Enraged beyond endurance, Washington ordered Jefferson, as secretary of state, to discipline "the French monkey"—Genêt was about half the president's height, with dark, dirty red hair, "coarse features," and a huge mouth. Jefferson took to his bed in a fit of cowardice, pleading migraine. The president sent him a searching letter: "Is the Minister of the French Republic to set the Acts of this Government at defiance, with impunity, and then threaten the executive with an appeal to the people? What must the world think of such conduct, and of the government of the United States for submitting to it?" Jefferson had no alternative but to resign (as of December 31, 1793), and at a cabinet meeting it was decided to demand Genêt's recall. Washington By Godded them all, said he would "rather be in his grave" than president and accused Jefferson and other critics of "an impudent desire to insult him." (In fact Genêt remained, for having received news he would be executed if he returned to France, he begged Washington for refugee status, which was grudgingly granted.)

Washington was in a self-assertive mood in 1793–94, unusual for him. He refused to allow the outfitting of French privateers in American ports. He resisted demands for commercial retaliation against British ships in response to the British seizure of American ships trading—against Washington's advice—with the French West Indies. When the Whiskey Rebellion came to a climax he not only put it down with enormous force (as noted earlier) but reviewed the troops, rode with them for a while, and later accused the Democratic Societies of inciting the tax evaders (another hit at Jefferson). He was clearly unhappy as well as angry. He said he was bitterly sorry he had agreed to serve a second term. He "had never repented but once the having slipped the moment of resigning his office, *and that was every moment since.*" He appointed Edmund Jennings Randolph to succeed Jefferson, but turned on him when an intercepted message appeared to show Randolph accepting bribes in return for pushing American policy in a French direction. Having treated Randolph with great deviousness—Washington could be two-faced when he chose—he suddenly accused him of treason: "By the Eternal God . . .

the damndest liar on the face of the earth!" The disgrace of Randolph, almost certainly innocent, was a rare example of Washington behaving unjustly, and reflects his frustrations, caused more than by anything else by the endless snipings in the press. Among other things, it accused him of drawing more than his salary, of favoring a shameless agreement with England, and of being "the stepfather of his country."

The fury had one positive outcome: Washington determined to come to a final settlement with the British and sent the chief justice, John Jay, a leading New York Federalist, to London to discuss terms and, not least, avert a war with Britain, on which Jefferson and his friends had set their radical hearts. Jay was primarily a politician who was to resign in 1795 to run for the governorship of New York. His political acumen is why Washington made him chief justice in the first place, seeing the post as akin to the English lord chancellor, who usually sat in cabinet. It is a valid criticism of Washington (and of the Founding Fathers as a whole) that they gave insufficient thought to the third branch of the state, the judiciary. They left it to the first Congress, which duly produced a 1789 Judiciary Act. It was written, with Washington's strong approval, by Oliver Ellsworth, author of the Connecticut Compromise, to whom the president was grateful. It created, in record time, a federal system of courts, which has remained virtually unchanged in more than two centuries. Unfortunately, because Washington and his advisers were brought up in the English common law tradition, where judges interpreted law all the time, and made it, they failed to realize the importance of judicial review (and the accompanying power to order federal officials to carry out judicial instructions) under a written constitution. This failure had momentous consequences for the future, especially in the twentieth century—indeed, they began to manifest themselves early in the nineteenth under Chief Justice Marshall, who used judicial review to construct the legal framework of American capitalism. If Washington had been aware of the possibilities of judge-made law he would have recoiled in horror. But his eye was never on this particular ball. He sent Jay to London precisely because he was a political lawyer capable of doing a tricky diplomatic job.

Jay came back with what Washington considered a good treaty, good because fair to both sides and therefore likely to last. But nothing in his presidency gave him more trouble. The treaty provided for British evacuation of the Northwest ports, thus at last making possible the full settlement of the Ohio valley, something dear to the president's heart. It opened up the British West Indies to U.S. vessels. It gave the United States "most favored nation" status in British trade. It enormously increased American exports to Britain and her possessions and British exports to America (thus boosting revenue from Hamilton's import duties). It is hard to think of any treaty that benefited both signatories more. Washington was delighted, and sent his London minister plenipotentiary, Thomas Pinckney, to Madrid to negotiate a comparable arrangement with Spain. This also succeeded, giving America access to the Mississippi valley through New Orleans and acknowledgment by Spain of her boundary claims east of the great river, and in east and west Florida. By these two treaties all the last remaining obstacles to full-scale American westward expansion into the Ohio and Mississippi valleys were finally removed, thus crowning Washington's life work.

The president, therefore, was understandably furious when Jefferson and his press pack, speaking for the French lobby, denounced the treaty as a sellout to British interests. Washington got the Jay treaty text on March 7, 1795, and had it ratified by the Senate in a secret debate on June 25, publishing it the following month. Despite the subsequent uproar, he signed it in August. And he got the Senate to ratify the Spanish treaty March 3, 1796. But he was outraged again on March 24 when the House voted for all the secret papers connected with the Jay treaty to be published. He flatly refused, pleading executive privilege in maintaining the privacy of diplomatic correspondence. As a result, he had to fight a strenuous behind-the-scenes battle to get the House to vote funds to implement the Jay treaty, which it grudgingly did on April 30 by a narrow majority. By this time Washington was heartily sick of politics and office and began to draft his resignation address. Hamilton, no longer in government but still his closest adviser, polished it in May and it was published in the *American Daily Advertiser* of Philadelphia.

This noble document, primarily the work of the president himself, as his draft shows, is a wise and pungent piece of final advice from a successful general and superb statesman to a nation he had made free and set upon the path of self-government and huge prosperity. It is a powerful, at times passionate, plea for national unity, against the spirit of party (particularly if founded on geographical basis), for complete freedom of action on the international scene, and avoidance of entangling alliances. It laid down the master plan for American expansion and advancement until well into the twentieth century, when modernity finally overthrew the tyranny of distance, and America had to enter the world, for the first time, as a participant in all its troubles. It must be read in full, and is worth reading in full: every American schoolchild ought to be familiar with its text, which has much more relevance to the present day than the Declaration of Independence itself. It is an extraordinary climax to Washington's public career and a fitting and elegant conclusion to his efforts to make America free, contented, prosperous, and strong.

The address was not without a strong religious note. Washington spoke to "friends and fellow-citizens." He was talking to Congress, and through Congress as a body to all the individuals who made up the nation. He said he could not have done what he did to free and build the nation without a consciousness of their support. "Profoundly penetrated with this idea," he said,

I shall carry it with me to my grave, as a strong incitement to unceasing vows that Heaven may continue to you the choicest tokens of its beneficence; that your Union and brother affection may be perpetual; that the free Constitution, which is the work of your hands, may be sacredly maintained; that its Administration in every department may be stamped with Wisdom and Virtue; that, in fine, the happiness of the people of these States, under the auspices of liberty, may be made complete by so careful and preservative and so prudent a use of this blessing as will acquire to them the glory of recommending it to the applause, the affection, the adoption of every nation which is yet a stranger to it.

Thus, having recommended the American pattern of government to the world, Washington concluded his public life. He stayed in Philadelphia to see his successor, John Adams, inaugurated on March 4, 1797, and was back in Mount Vernon, profoundly relieved and grateful, ten days later.

Chapter Seven

Last Years

W ASHINGTON'S FINAL RETIREMENT was not long, a mere three years. But he enjoyed it despite anxieties. His step-grandson, George Washington Parke Custis, did badly at Princeton. The general paid his debts and gave him advice. He was to stop wasting his time by "running up and down stairs" and keeping in "conversation anyone who will talk to you." He should get up early, study between breakfast and dinner, walk until tea, and study again until bedtime. He must be punctual for meals, since the servants had "to be running here and there and they know not where, to summon you." He could hunt on Saturdays. Washington's own day was regular in the extreme. Rise at five A.M., read or write until seven. Breakfast of tea and corn muffins spread with butter and honey. Then by horse to the endless inspection of fields. Return at two, dress, dinner;

if there were guests he chatted to them afterward over a glass of Madeira. Then read the newspapers, getting ten in all, and writing letters. Tea at seven; then talk till nine, and bed.

Jefferson spread the rumor that the "old man" was senile—had been, in fact, since 1793 (when they had first quarreled over France). But Washington's letters and a mass of other documents show he was sharp, hard working, and observant right to the end. He had hoped to proceed with his schemes of liberating his slaves. In some cases he had already done so: he left behind half his black slaves in Philadelphia so that they could automatically become free. But his plans to sell outlying lands for this purpose, to rent most of the Mount Vernon estates to capable farmers who would retain former slaves as free hired hands, all failed for lack of buyers and tenants. He continued to supervise directly twelve square miles of land, no easy job for a man over sixty-five. But visitors testified to the splendor of Mount Vernon, its spectacular green lawn in the front and "perhaps the most beautiful view in the world" from the loggia. The house and gardens were comparable to "the most beautiful examples of the great old houses of England." Vast fields of corn, wheat, alfalfa, flax, peas, and rye were nearby. The mill with a new and modern mechanism "functioned magnificently." A distillery turned out twelve thousand gallons of whiskey a year and "delicate and succulent" feed for 150 enormous pigs "so excessively bulky that they can hardly drag their big bellies on the ground." There were six hundred sheep. The imported jackass now had fifty mule descendants. Washington had designed an ingenious plough he showed visitors and a new octagonal barn. He was again involved in river and canal plans.

Nor were the sterner duties of the state neglected by the old warrior. A family portrait survives of Washington, in retirement, surrounded by his family. But he wears full uniform. Was this a symbolic gesture indicating his willingness—and readiness—to return to arms the moment his country needed him? It is rather a reference to an actual recall to arms in 1798 when war with France threatened. President Adams decided to expand the army and, on the significant date of July 4, he commissioned Washington as lieutenant-general and commander in chief. Washington was not consulted before the announcement was made and resented being brought down a grade in rank. The business produced the last serious row of his life. He wanted both Hamilton and Knox to join him and General Charles Pinckney as his number two. He argued that the last was "an officer of his military repute, fond of the Profession, spirited, active and judicious." Moreover, "His connections are numerous, powerful and more influential than any other in the three Southern States." The southern point was important because "If the French should be so mad as openly and formidably to invade these United States . . . their operations will commence in the Southern quarters; because it is the weakest; because they will expect, from the tenor of debates in Congress to find more friends there; because there can be no doubt of their assuming our own negroes against us; and because they will be more contiguous to their Islands and Louisiana." The letter shows the Old Man still thinking clearly and strategically, and his approach contrasted sharply with the muddled

noises from the president. Adams hastily sent to the Senate, for con-
firmation, the names of Hamilton as inspector-general (number
two), and Pinckney and Knox as major-generals. As a result, all three
raised objections and Washington had to exercise all his admirable
patience and skill in writing conciliatory letters to them and others.
The row took it out of him. He fell ill with fever, and his weight sank
from its usual 220 pounds to 190 pounds. He managed, nonetheless,
to go to Philadelphia in November to direct the war preparations. He
found things in confusion but contrived to produce two memoranda,
totaling eight thousand words. They were two of the best state
papers he ever wrote, and all his work, for he apologized for the
crossings out—he had not time to have them copied by Lear. On
December 14, he left for home, this time for good.

His chief concern now was to settle his will and, in particular,
provide for the liberating of his slaves after Martha's death. The
thing had become an obsession. As he explained in the text: "Upon
the decease of my wife it is my Will and desire that all the slaves
which I hold *in my own right* shall receive their freedom. To eman-
cipate them during her life would, tho' earnestly wished by me, be attended with such insuperable difficulties on account of their
intermixture by Marriages with the Dower Negroes [Martha's], as to
excite the most painful sensations, if not disagreeable consequences
from the latter, while both descriptions are in the occupancy of the
same Proprietor; it not being in my power, under the tenure by which
the Dower Negroes are held, to manumit them." There followed detailed provisions about the feeding and clothing of manumitted

slaves unable to support themselves, the education of the young, and the upkeep of orphans. He added: "And I do hereby expressly forbid the sale, or transportation out of the said Commonwealth [of Virginia] of any Slave I may die possessed of, under any preference whatsoever." This insistence reflected his knowledge that the fate all slaves most feared was the splitting up of families by auction and "selling down the river" to the Deep South. That is what happened to Jefferson's unfortunate slaves: after a lifetime spent attacking slavery verbally, Jefferson left such enormous debts that his heirs felt they had no alternative but to sell all his slaves, men, women, and children for what they would fetch in the market. Happily, Washington's debts, "of which there are few, and none of magnitude," as the will states, could be paid out of ready cash. The paragraph on slaves, the most important in the will (except the preceding one, which left his estate to Martha during her life), included solemn admonitions to his executors to do exactly what he laid down about the slaves—it was to be "religiously fulfilled . . . without evasion, neglect or delay." There was also special provision for William Lee, his faithful rider to foxhounds and in battle.

The will, as might have been expected, was careful, detailed, fair, and just, and seems to have been written by the general himself, with legal help. Appended to it was a schedule of his property, totaling ninety-six square miles, which he had been at pains to compile. This is an astonishingly accurate and detailed document, and showed that Washington died owning $530,000 in land and stock alone, making him one of the richest men in America.

The general worked until the end. He often went to the Washington site, to see how his capital city was progressing. He wanted it to have its own university (a growing concern for educating the young properly was a feature of his last years), for which he made provision in his will. He wrote letters on the army and on naval matters. He took an intense interest in the warlike proceedings of France, where Bonaparte was pushing his way to the top. One of his last letters (to Hamilton) concerns the creation of an army academy. His home was always full of family and friends. He continued his daily inspection of his farms on horseback, whatever the weather, the last being on December 13, 1799. He returned wet, with snow in his hair, and was too tired to change for dinner. Early the following morning he complained of fever and was unable to drink. Much bled, by himself and the doctors, in accordance with the primitive medical knowledge of the day, he died while taking his own pulse, about ten o'clock that night. He was buried in the Gothic-style family vault he had prepared in the garden at Mount Vernon, on December 18, aged sixty-seven.

One of his later visitors, who spent a day at the house in the general's company, was young Copley, son of the Anglo-American painter John Singleton Copley. It is a thousand pities that old Copley, by far the best American portraitist of the age, never got the chance of a sitting. But his son left a vignette. Copley was to become Lord Lyndhurst, three times Lord Chancellor of England, to sit in cabinet with Wellington and Peel; he was the close friend of Disraeli, knew Gladstone and Macaulay, Dickens, Thackeray, Scott, and the young Tennyson. He met everyone of distinction in Europe from Talleyrand to Goethe. Yet, when old and retired, he said that meeting Washington was the greatest privilege he had enjoyed and that the day at Mount Vernon was the most remarkable in his entire life.

Bibliography

The standard work is Douglas Southall Freeman, *George Washington: A Biography* (7 vols., New York, 1948–57). Of recent works, the best is Harrison Clark, *All Cloudless Glory: The Life of George Washington* (2 vols., Washington, D.C. 1995). This work is particularly important in exposing forgeries of letters, of which there are many. Also recommended is Richard Norton Smith, *Patriarch: George Washington and the New American Nation* (Boston, 1993). Richard Brookhiser, *Founding Father: Rediscovering George Washington* (New York, 1996) is a short, provocative treatment. Henry Wiencek, *An Imperfect God: George Washington, His Slaves, and the Creation of America* (New York, 2003), deals with the controversial subject of his slaveholdings. Miriam Anne Bourne, *First Family: George Washington and his Intimate Relations* (New York, 1982), discusses his extended family. For the intellectual background, useful books are Garry Wills, *Cincinnatus: George Washington and the Enlightenment* (New York, 1984), and Louis Martin Sears, *George Washington and the French Revolution* (Detroit, 1960). Emily Stone Whiteley, *Washington and his Aides-de-Camp* (New York, 1936), deals with his military family. David Hackett Fischer, *Washington's Crossing* (Oxford 2004), is a good recent treatment of the Revolutionary War. On Mount Vernon, see R. F. Dalzell and L. B. Dalzell, *George Washington's Mount Vernon* (New York, 1998). The most useful collection of letters, diaries, and speeches is John Rhodehamel, ed., *George Washington: Writings* (New York, 1997), which also has a full chronology.